Introduction

The units in this Workbook supplement and review those in the *First Language English for Cambridge IGCSE Student Book*. Each unit contains different sections focusing on language skills. The **Reading** sections contain a wide variety of texts, including blogs, news and feature articles, autobiography and fiction. After each passage there are exam-style questions. The **Using English** sections give the opportunity for grammar and spelling practice; there are also vocabulary and language awareness exercises to help you improve all your language skills. The **Writing** sections include useful information on writing **Compositions** and on **Directed Writing** tasks, where you are asked to read a passage and use that information to write in a specified style, for example a speech, interview, letter or article.

The Cambridge IGCSE® First Language English syllabus is designed to help you develop your ability to communicate clearly, accurately and effectively in both speech and writing. To this end, this Workbook will help you to develop a wider vocabulary and use grammar, spelling and punctuation accurately in your written work. This will help you to communicate appropriately and effectively; it will also influence your personal writing style for narrative and descriptive essays.

As you develop your reading skills, you will also be improving your analytical skills, learning how to analyse texts and infer what is written between the lines, and how to order facts and present opinions politely and effectively. All students preparing for English exams should try to read widely to improve their awareness of how English can be used for different purposes, for example, to inform or entertain. Reading stories from different English-speaking countries will broaden your vocabulary and cultural knowledge. Reading stories from different periods in time will show you how people thought, spoke and behaved in the past. Reading online newspapers will keep you up to date with what is happening in the world for class discussions or debates, discursive essays or coursework assignments. Reading widely helps you to become aware of register and of how English is used in different contexts.

1

Travellers' tales

Writing skills questionnaire

1. Tick the writing activities below that you like doing.

    ☐ Writing stories

    ☐ Descriptive writing (to inform and entertain)

    ☐ Writing informative or discursive essays (to argue a point)

    ☐ Writing History, Geography or Business Studies essays

    ☐ Writing up experiments

    ☐ Writing articles for the school magazine or English lessons

    ☐ Writing long emails to friends

    ☐ Writing playscripts

    ☐ Texting

    ☐ Keeping a diary or writing a blog

2. Write answers to the following questions about what and how you write.

    a. Think about what you write on a daily basis. Apart from essays for school, what else do you write most days?

    ....

b. Do you consciously change your style for different writing activities? Give an example.

....

c. Choose two styles of writing that you use and explain how they differ (e.g. texting and essays).

....

d. Now think about your thinking skills. Are you aware of thinking in different ways when you write? If the answer is 'yes', how and why does your way of thinking change?

....

....

e. What different writing styles do you need to use in school subjects other than English?

....

....

f. Are there any writing activities that you do at school that you expect to use after you leave school?

....

g. Look at the writing styles you ticked in question 1. Choose one you are good at and/or enjoy. Explain what you like about it.

....

....

h. Do you think you will ever write for pleasure after you leave school, college or university? Explain why or why not.

....

....

i. Why do you think you have to learn how to write in different styles in English lessons?

....

....

j. "Learning to write a good summary is the most useful skill you'll ever learn." Do you agree or disagree? Explain your thoughts.

....

....

Answering Reading questions

navigational dividers (n): a device like a compass used for making or calculating measurements at sea.

In this book, you will be asked to read passages of various lengths that have been written in different styles for a range of purposes. You will then be asked questions on the information they contain and on how the texts have been written.

Read the following passage carefully and answer the questions that follow.

Mystery of Alexander Selkirk, the real Robinson Crusoe, solved

By Richard Alleyne, *Daily Telegraph* (30 October 2008)

It may have taken nearly 300 years but archaeologists have finally confirmed the campsite of castaway Alexander Selkirk, thought to be the inspiration for Robinson Crusoe.

Scottish sailor Selkirk was marooned on a small tropical island in the Pacific for more than four years.

Cast away on a desert island, surviving on what nature alone can provide, praying for rescue but at the same time fearing the sight of a boat on the horizon. These are the imaginative creations of Daniel Defoe in his famous novel *Robinson Crusoe*.

But the story is believed to be based on the real-life experience of Scottish sailor Selkirk, marooned in 1704 on a small tropical island in the Pacific for more than four years, and now archaeological evidence has been found to support his existence on the island.

An article in the journal *Post-Medieval Archaeology* claims that an archaeological dig on the Argentinian island of Aguas Buenas, 470 miles off the Chilean coast, reveals evidence of the campsite of an early European occupant. The most compelling evidence is the discovery of a fragment of a pair of navigational dividers which could only have belonged to a ship's master or navigator, which historical evidence suggests Selkirk must have been.

Selkirk's rescuer, Captain Woodes Rogers' account of what he saw on arrival at Aguas Buenas in 1709 lists "some practical pieces" and mathematical instruments amongst the few possessions that Selkirk had taken with him from the ship.

Dr David Caldwell, National Museums Scotland, who helped lead the dig, said the find finally confirmed the whereabouts of the castaway camp.

"The evidence uncovered at Aguas Buenas corroborates the stories of Alexander Selkirk's stay on the island and provides a fascinating insight into his existence there," he said. "I am satisfied in my mind that this is the place where Selkirk set up his camp. I never thought we had a chance of finding it but the discovery of the divider was crucial."

The finds also provide an insight into exactly how Selkirk might have lived on the island.

Postholes suggest he built two shelters near to a freshwater stream and had access to a viewpoint over the harbour from where he would be able to watch for approaching ships and ascertain whether they were friend or foe. Accounts written shortly after his rescue describe him shooting goats with a gun rescued from the ship and eventually learning to outrun them, eating their meat and using their skins as clothing.

[…] Alexander Selkirk was born in the small seaside town of Lower Largo, Fife, Scotland in 1676. A younger son of a shoemaker, he was drawn to a life at sea from an early age. In 1704, during a privateering voyage on the Cinque Ports, Selkirk fell out with the commander over the ship's seaworthiness and he decided to remain behind on an island, now named Robinson Crusoe, where they had landed to overhaul the worm-infested vessel. He cannot have known that it would be five years before he was picked up by an English ship visiting the island.

1. Answer the following questions in full sentences.

   a. What is the "compelling evidence" mentioned in line 25?

....

....

   b. Suggest another word or phrase the writer could have used instead of "compelling" in line 25.

....

....

   c. Why is this evidence "compelling"?

....

....

   d. In line 46 the writer says the discovery of the "divider was crucial". Explain why.

....

....

   e. Name another "find" (line 47) that was important to the archaeologists.

....

....

2. Using the article on Alexander Selkirk for information, complete the chart below.

Alexander Selkirk	Information in the text
Where he came from	
Biographical details	
Where he was marooned	
What he had with him on the island	
How he passed his time	
His rescue	
Other interesting details	

Answering summary questions

Answering summary questions gives you the opportunity to demonstrate your skills in making notes and summarising in continuous writing.

1. Make notes in response to the question.

   a. Keyword the question. For example, complete the keywording that has been started below.

      Summarise the **conditions** and the **evidence** found on Aguas Buenas Island that may explain how Alexander Selkirk survived there alone for four years.

   b. Re-read the whole passage on page 6 and identify information that is relevant to the question. (You may only need certain paragraphs, not the whole passage.) Annotate the text as you go along to help you to locate information later. Some examples are given below. Look at how the student has found, deduced and labelled information.

Cast away on a desert island, surviving on what nature alone can provide, praying for rescue but at the same time fearing the sight of a boat on 5 the horizon. These are the imaginative creations of Daniel Defoe in his famous novel *Robinson Crusoe*.

But the story is believed 10 to be based on the real-life experience of Scottish sailor Selkirk, marooned in 1704 on a small tropical island in the Pacific for more than four years, 15 and now archaeological evidence has been found to support his existence on the island.

An article in the journal *Post-Medieval Archaeology* 20 claims that an archaeological dig on the Argentinian island of Aguas Buenas, 470 miles off the Chilean coast, reveals evidence of the campsite of an early 25 European occupant …

> tropical – so probably had fruit and berries, and not very cold at night

> lived off the land (and sea) – Aguas Buenas (good water?)

> wood to make a fire

   c. In the passage on page 6 there are eight significant points on Alexander Selkirk and how he may have survived on Aguas Buenas Island. Write the eight points below in note form. (You do not need to use proper sentences.)

   - ....
   - ....
   - ....
   - ....
   - ....
   - ....
   - ....
   - ....

   d. Before you can write your summary, you need to organise your notes. Number them in a logical sequence in order to respond to the question.

2. Now use your notes to summarise how Alexander Selkirk may have survived for over four years alone on Aguas Buenas Island. Your summary should contain all eight points in your notes.

Use your own words as far as possible and continuous writing (not note form). Write between 100 and 150 words. Use a separate sheet of paper if necessary.

....

....

....

....

....

....

....

....

....

....

....

....

....

....

....

....

....

....

....

....

....

....

....

....

....

....

Improving narrative writing skills

Writing Compositions is your opportunity to demonstrate your knowledge of different writing styles, your personal writing skills (including use of English and vocabulary) and your technical accuracy (grammar and spelling).

1. Read the following points on how to write good **narrative compositions**. Then choose one of the questions on the next page.

   - Choose a question you will enjoy writing and/or you can do well.

   - Read and keyword the question carefully. Note that you may be asked to write just the beginning or the end of a story, or just one episode (a scene) from it.

   - Even if you only have to write an episode or the beginning of a story, plan your storyline and decide how the episode ends before you begin. The end of a story may come as a surprise to the reader, but the writer should know exactly what is going to happen. A good narrative builds up to a climax and leads towards a conclusion.

   Some good stories start with a framing device such as a frightening flashback or someone telling the story to listeners, but do not attempt this if it is not appropriate to the question or could confuse the reader. Never end a story with *and then I woke up* or *It was all a dream*.

   - If you are writing an episode, the beginning or the end of a story, you do not need a beginning/middle/end format.

   - Keep the storyline simple but try to vary the pace of the narrative: if it is too slow it will become boring; too fast and it will become confusing.

   - Decide on the tense you are going to use. Narrative compositions are usually written in the past tense, but could also be written in the present tense.

   - Decide on the narrative voice (who is telling the story), whether you want to write in the first person (*I/we*) or third person (*he/she/it*). Do not change the narrative viewpoint (voice) once you have begun.

   - Keep the number of characters to a minimum to avoid confusion. Bring characters and places to life with interesting details so the reader can imagine them in his or her mind's eye.

   - Not all characters need dialogue. Too much dialogue will turn the story into a play so avoid giving characters trivial things to say. Indent dialogue like starting a new paragraph and punctuate direct speech accurately. Also find alternatives for *he/she said*.

   - Use figurative language in your description with interesting metaphors and similes. Avoid over-used comparisons and clichés.

   - Proofread and edit your composition. Silly mistakes ruin any form of writing. Professional authors write numerous drafts and edit them carefully. In an exam you do not have time to do this, but you must always leave time to read through and correct what you have written before it is handed in.

2. Write between 350 and 450 words on **one** of the following:

"Castaway" Write an episode of a story in which a character is marooned on a desert island.

OR

"Home at last!" Write the end of a story where the main character returns home after being away for a long period of time.

Use a separate sheet of paper if necessary.

....
....
....
....
....
....
....
....
....
....
....
....
....
....
....
....
....
....
....
....
....
....
....
....
....
....
....
....

The world of nature

Reading skills questionnaire

1. Look at the following types of text and think about the ways you might read them.

Type of text	Active reading	Passive reading
Clocks		
Ingredients listed on a food product label		
Cereal packets on the breakfast table		
Recipes		
Mobile phone texts		
Instructions for your mobile phone		
First page of a novel		
Email from a friend		
Exam questions		
Newspaper headlines		
Magazines in waiting rooms		
Interesting magazine articles		

2. Which of the above texts require active reading skills where you have to read each word or item of data carefully? Tick them in the 'Active reading' column.

3. Which texts can you read passively, without thinking about what you are reading too much? Tick them in the 'Passive reading' column.

Remember that you can read some texts in both ways, depending on the situation or your level of interest.

Improving reading skills

Good reading skills are essential for success in English. Through reading you can understand how and why a text was written and this will help you to develop and improve your own writing skills. Even passive reading improves vocabulary, grammar and your speaking and listening skills. Active reading improves life skills and will therefore help you in all your school subjects.

You can use different levels of reading according to what you need to know. You may glance through a magazine and skim titles, headlines or subheadings until you find something of interest; then, depending how much you want to know or how challenging the vocabulary is, you read the actual text with a greater level of attention. In exams with a choice of question, you probably skim through the questions until you find one you can answer well and then read the instructions for that question carefully to understand what you need to do.

Skimming and scanning

Skimming is reading quickly to get the gist of what a text is about. Your eye skims words and illustrations to give you an idea of what it is about.

Scanning is reading to locate specific information or details.

Close reading and keywording questions

Once you have chosen your question in an exam, it is vital to re-read it very carefully. You need to understand precisely what you are being asked to do: keyword the question by selecting the important (key) words that tell you what to do and what to include in your answer.

Close reading and analysing texts

You also need to use close reading skills to analyse texts to find out how they have been written.

Close reading is sometimes called textual analysis because it examines the writer's style, vocabulary and use of language and analyses the effects on the reader. For example, when you think about advertisements, ask yourself: How has the advertiser tried to influence me?

Scanning

Read this article about butterflies and do the reading activities that follow.

Warm spring brings bumper year for Britain's butterflies

By Sarah Morrison, *The Independent* (7 June 2011)

The tiny Lulworth Skipper was spotted in April in Dorset, seven weeks early.

British butterflies are expected in spectacular abundance this year, with more than a quarter of all species native to the isles having made their earliest recorded appearances as a result of the warmest spring for 351 years. 5

Fifteen British butterfly types have appeared weeks before they would have done a decade ago, with conservationists already comparing 2011 to 1893, a landmark for early sightings of the insects. 10

Of the 59 resident and regular migrant species, 53 have been seen, an occurrence called "exceptional" by Butterfly Conservation's chief executive Martin Warren. 15

One of the smallest butterflies, the orange Lulworth Skipper, was spotted on 28 April in south Dorset, seven weeks before expected and the earliest since records began. The Small Copper, bright copper with brown spots and an occasional 20 visitor to gardens in May, was seen on 9 March in Lincolnshire, six weeks earlier than normal and two-and-a-half weeks ahead of its previous record in 2007.

The rare round-edged Wood White, usually 25 found in woodland glades by the end of May, emerged in the third week of April in Shropshire and Sussex, five weeks early.

The Dingy Skipper, Grizzled Skipper, Brimstone, Green-veined White, Orange-tip, 30 Black Hairstreak, Duke of Burgundy, White Admiral, Pearl-bordered Fritillary, High Brown Fritillary, Dark Green Fritillary and Silver-washed Fritillary all appeared on average three weeks before they did in the 1990s, according to records. 35

For Dr Warren, the trend is "almost certainly" linked to rising temperatures. "Some butterflies are spreading north due to climate change, which is fantastic, as we are seeing beautiful butterflies, like the Speckled Wood and Orange-tip, which we 40 didn't see 20 or 30 years ago, in Scotland."

But Matthew Oates, naturalist for the National Trust, warned: "Some of these species are coming out before their nectar sources are present, so will the food available be suitable and will there be 45 anything for the caterpillars to eat?"

1. Scan the article about butterflies in Britain to find relevant information to complete the sentences below. Use numbers only. The first one has been done for you.

   a. The spring of 2011 was the warmest spring in Britain for ...*351*... years.

   b. .... types of butterfly appeared many weeks before they would have done .... years ago.

   c. .... of the .... resident and migrant species were sighted earlier than normal.

   d. The orange Lulworth Skipper was spotted .... weeks earlier than usual.

   e. The Speckled Wood and Orange-tip were not seen in Scotland .... or .... years ago.

Improving summarising skills

When summarising information you have heard, read or been told you probably generalise, leaving out specific details. However, it is not always possible to generalise facts, times or important data so you need to find a way to include them as concisely as possible.

Answer the following summary question on the article on British butterflies. Include facts, times and relevant data about the butterflies in as few words as possible.

Summarise why butterflies are arriving in Britain earlier than in the past and why this is potentially threatening to the different species.

1. Make notes on why butterflies are arriving in Britain earlier than they used to. Include information on:

    • the early arrival of butterflies

    • the weather

    • the availability of food.

   There are five main points. Write your notes in the lines provided. (You do not have to write in complete sentences.)

   • ....

   • ....

   • ....

   • ....

   • ....

2. Summarise why butterflies are arriving in Britain earlier than in the past and why this is potentially threatening to the different species.

   Use your own words as far as possible and continuous writing (not note form). Write no more than 100 words. Use a separate sheet of paper if necessary.

Descriptive writing (1)

Here are two descriptions of riverside settings: one is in Australia, the other in England. Read the descriptions below carefully, then do the descriptive writing activity that follows.

Passage A: New South Wales, Australia, 1813

By the time the sun was lighting up the topmost leaves of the forest, he was away a ways up the valley. It was a still and silent place. The water, although clear, was as brown as strong tea. On either side mangroves masked the banks. Beyond was a narrow strip of level ground where river-oaks hung, and then the ridges 5 angled up, steep and stony on either side.

    The mosquitoes were ferocious. Thornhill watched a big one with striped legs land on his arm and push its needle-like biting part against the stuff of his shirt until it bent. Somewhere ahead of him at the top of a tree, a bird made a measured silvery sound 10 again and again, a little bell being struck. A fish launched itself out of the water and through the air in a flash of silver muscle. The place held its breath, watching.

From *The Secret River*, by Kate Grenville

Coot: a small, dark grey water bird with a white mark on its head.

Passage B: Cornwall, England, 1913

A roll of thick white mist curled around the many cornered house, sidled up the chimneys and settled down to await the sun. Below, between high willow herb and tall rushes, the old river barely moved. A late night water rat cut his way home through the shallows. An early rising trout snapped a fly. Along the waterside, 5 the never quiet ducks pattered and chattered. Coots gathered food among the reeds. A heron speared an unwary amphibian for breakfast. Morning had come to a slow turn in a Tamar valley.

From *The Magpie*, by J.G. Harlond

1. Write a paragraph describing a peaceful place. Use the planning grid below to help you.

    Include the following information.
    *   Where: setting and the description of the place
    *   When: the time of day
    *   Who: presence or absence of people
    *   How: imagery and figurative language (simile/metaphor)
    *   Effect: how you see or imagine each place

Setting	
Time	
People	
Imagery	
Figurative language	
Desired effect(s) on reader	

2. Write a paragraph describing a tranquil place you know (it does not have to be near a river). Include the following:

    *   setting (time and place)
    *   atmosphere
    *   descriptive imagery.

    Use a separate sheet of paper if necessary.

REMINDER

Remember to use your five senses in descriptive writing. Think about how you want your reader to interpret what you have written.

....

....

....

....

....

....

....

....

....

....

....

....

Improving descriptive writing skills (2)

You may choose to write a narrative (see page 11) or a descriptive composition in your exam or for your Coursework Portfolio.

1. Read the following points on how to write good **descriptive compositions**. Then answer the question that follows.

   A descriptive composition is not a story; it does not need a beginning, middle and an end. Give your description a framework, such as a clear setting or location in time, to create a structure, but do not create a storyline. If you are writing about a street market, for instance, you can be walking through the market or watching from an outdoor café, but you do not need to invent a dramatic incident.

   • Write about something you know well or have seen or felt in detail.

   • Use interesting, unusual vocabulary and a variety of sentence structures. For example, be precise when you describe colour: red can be blood-red or bright scarlet; green can be sea-green, apple-green or the colour of new-mown grass. Don't repeat words: find synonyms or alternative ways to express what you are seeing, thinking or feeling.

   • Try to use all five senses to give the reader a clear sense of the location, event and/or atmosphere. Include interesting, unusual or amusing details.

   • Avoid using clichés or overused, childish vocabulary such as *nice*, *little*, *old*, *big*, *good*, *bad*. Descriptive writing gives you a chance to show off your vocabulary, so use it!

2. Read the passage below about a rain storm in India.

Rain!

As it does every year, the wind has blown steadily out of the south-west, rolling its cargo of doughy air across the plain to slap hard against the mountains. For days, weeks, the air has funnelled upwards, cooling as it rises, spinning vast towers of condensation over the peaks. Now these hanging gardens of cloud have ripened to the point where they can no longer maintain themselves.

So, the rain.

It falls first over the mountains, an unimaginable shock of water. Caught in the open, herdsmen and woodcutters pull their shawls over their heads and run for shelter. Then in a chain reaction, cloud speaking to cloud, the rain rolls over the foothills, dousing fires, battering on roofs, bringing smiles to the faces of the people who run outside to greet it, the water for which they have been waiting so long.

From *The Impressionist*, by Hari Kunzru

3. Write about rain, a rainy day or the absence of rain in your country.

   Make your composition as descriptive as possible by using the five senses. Write between 350 and 450 words. Use a separate sheet of paper if necessary.

3 Points of view

Looking for evidence

Read the extract on the following pages from the historical novel *Catching the Eagle* by Karen Charlton, then answer the questions that follow.

The story is based on what happened to one of the author's family in 1809 and is set in a rural area of Northumberland in northern England. In this scene a detective from London named Stephen Lavender and his assistant, Police Constable Woods, visit the cottage of a day labourer named Jamie Charlton. They are investigating the theft of over a thousand pounds in cash and paper bills from Kirkley Hall. Charlton, who was working at the Hall on the day of the robbery, is suspected of taking the money.

13 April 1809

The trap drew up outside Charlton's stone cottage. They could see it was a modest home of only a couple of rooms, with an overgrown garden to the front. The budding stems and brown thorns of a climbing rose clambered up the wall beside the 5 partially open door. A spiral of smoke curled away from the chimney into the clear blue sky above. The delightful smell of freshly baked bread wafted in their direction.

"Well, at least there's someone at home," 10 Woods observed.

They climbed down stiffly from the swaying vehicle, and sent a flurry of chickens squawking along the dusty track and onto the rickety fence which surrounded the tangled garden. In the 15 tumbling confusion of daffodils, herbs, currant bushes and vegetables, a child's face suddenly appeared, framed with red curls and a dirty white bonnet. Seconds later, up popped another – identical to the last. Both girls were wide-eyed, 20 and kneeling amongst the plants.

"What devil's trick is this!" the constable exclaimed.

Lavender smiled.

"Unusual isn't it? Twins rarely survive the 25 birth. Is your father at home, little miss?"

The child did not answer. Behind her, the gaping door swung open and a tall, very beautiful woman was framed in the doorway. She wiped her floury hands on her apron and pushed back a 30 wisp of gleaming, copper-coloured hair which had escaped from beneath her cap. Her large, green eyes flicked nervously across the faces of the two strange men before her.

"Are you wanting to see Jamie?" she asked. 35

"Mistress Charlton?" Lavender asked pleasantly. She nodded.

"We're looking for your husband, James Charlton. Is he at home?"

"He be out in the fields. Hannah, Mary – go 40 fetch your da."

The two girls needed no second bidding. They were up from their knees in a second, flew out of the gate and sped off towards the fields. Their boots clattered over the stony path and red 45 pigtails streamed behind them.

"Pretty gals, them," Woods observed.

"I'm Detective Lavender from Bow Street in London, Mistress Charlton. This is Constable Woods. We are investigating the theft of the rent 50 money from Kirkley Hall."

"You'd better come inside then," Cilla said calmly.

They followed her into the cottage. Lavender was keen to have a good look around before 55 Charlton arrived.

The door led straight into the main living area, which was dominated by the stone fireplace and a wooden table in the centre of the room. There was one padded armchair in front of the fire. 60 At the other side of the hearth stood an ancient yew settle, scattered with colourful homemade cushions. A soot-blackened rag rug lay on the floor. Along the entire back wall of the room was an oak dresser crammed and cluttered with pots, 65 pans, baking ingredients, knitting and sewing equipment and just about everything else the family owned. The table was covered with an appetising array of freshly made bread, pies and pastries. 70

Sitting on one of the wooden chairs at the table was a thin-faced woman who rose hurriedly as they entered.

"I'd best be getting along," she said.

"Take these into the bedroom, will you 75 Mary?" Cilla said quietly, ignoring her friend's embarrassment. She scooped up a pile of bulky brown paper parcels from the dresser and deposited them into the other woman's arms.

The woman pushed open the door on the back 80 wall with her foot and carried the parcels away. For a brief second, Lavender was able to see several beds in the darkened room. A man's coat hung on the outside of a wardrobe door.

Cilla now began to move the food from the 85 table into the space created on the dresser.

Lavender observed her dispassionately as she glided around the room. The faded blue dress she wore beneath her apron had lines of needle marks running from the dark stains beneath her armpits 90 down to her waist. It had obviously been let in and out several times – probably to accommodate her expanding waistline during pregnancies. As if on cue, an infant whimpered in the back room. She paused and listened but the sleepy child 95 seemed to settle again.

The woman was stunningly attractive but even in the darkened kitchen of the cottage he could see the fine lines around her eyes and the hint of grey at her temples. This magnificent red-headed 100 beauty was starting to lose her looks. How old would she be? Thirty perhaps? She was past her prime. Another five years of child-bearing, and the poverty and malnutrition which dogged her class would age her prematurely. 105

The woman Mary reappeared from the bedroom and moved towards the front door. She reached for her shawl from the back of the chair. Lavender and Woods stepped out of her way.

"I'll be seeing you, Cilla," she said as she left. 110 "Thank you for the money for the butter – I'll get you some change for that note as soon as I can." With this she gave Lavender and Woods a filthy look and then disappeared out of the cottage door.

Cilla gestured the men towards the spindly 115 chairs at the table.

"Take a seat," she said. "Jamie'll not be long; he's close by."

Lavender sat down and began to remove his gloves. He continued to scan the room. He saw 120 nothing unusual for a labourer's cottage: second-hand furniture, patched furnishings and pewter plates. There was another door off the kitchen which led to a small scullery. Cilla carried her baking implements into this side room [...] 125

This family eats well at the moment, he thought.

"Can I get you a cup of tea?" Cilla asked when she returned. The two men accepted and watched as she picked up a teaspoon and a battered, tin tea caddy. She measured out the 130 leaves carefully then dropped them into a chipped, brown teapot. Next she reached for the iron kettle which sat on the hearthstones and set it back over the fire to boil.

Suddenly, they heard voices and footsteps in 135 the garden outside. The light in the cottage dimmed as a tall, broad man paused into the doorway.

"Good morning, Mr. Charlton. I'm Detective Lavender from Bow Street in London. I've come 140 to ask you some questions about your movements on the day of the Kirkley Hall robbery."

Tea caddy: a container for tea leaves.

1. You are Detective Lavender. You think it is very probable that Jamie
    Charlton stole the money from Kirkley Hall. From memory, write down
    three items of evidence from the passage to suggest Charlton needs money.

    a. ....

    b. ....

    c. ....

2. You are Constable Woods. While you are at the cottage you make a
    list of evidence to suggest the Charlton family has recently acquired
    money. Re-read the passage and write down at least three points that
    demonstrate that Charlton has more money to spend than most poor
    folk in the area.

    ....

    ....

    ....

    ....

    ....

3. In those days a theft such as this was a hanging offence. Detective
    Lavender and Constable Woods need to be very sure of their facts
    before Charlton can be sent for trial. Is there any evidence in the
    passage to suggest Charlton may be innocent? Explain your thoughts.

    ....

    ....

    ....

4. You are Detective Lavender. Write a report for your superior in
    London explaining what you have seen at Charlton's cottage and why
    you want to stay in the area to make more enquiries. Write between
    250 and 350 words. Use a separate sheet of paper if necessary.

    Start like this:

    Report on Kirkley Hall robbery, Northumberland,
    14 April 1809

    On the 13 April, the home of James Charlton was visited
    prior to his interrogation.

    It is evident from this visit that...

    ....

    ....

    ....

    ....

    ....

    ....

Using English: register

Register is the word for the style of language you use in a given situation or for a particular subject matter.

Decide whether the register in each of the following sentences is formal, neutral or informal.

	Formal	Neutral	Informal
a. There's this kid called Joey see and he's hanging around waiting for a bus.			
b. Further to my letter dated 13 November, I request once again that you review the situation regarding our invoice.			
c. "Now, I would like everyone to take a seat and listen carefully to what I'm going to say."			

Using English: informal to formal

Rewrite these informal sentences in a more formal register. Make use of the verb in brackets in your sentence in the appropriate tense: past, present or future.

1. It was Tom that did all the graffiti, but they're going to let him off this time if he cleans it all off himself. (to punish)

   ....

   ....

2. Tom's been made to say sorry for the mess he's made of the wall. (to apologise)

   ....

   ....

3. Jim's dad says he'll make Jim join the Army if he doesn't get a job as soon as he leaves school. (to force)

   ....

   ....

4. My parents never let me stay up late on school nights. (to permit)

   ....

   ....

5. My mum says I have to help out with the housework if I want pocket money. (to oblige)

   ....

   ....

Improving directed writing skills: point of views

In Directed Writing or your Coursework Portfolio you should demonstrate that you know how to write clearly, accurately and effectively in an argumentative, persuasive or discursive style. Many of the guidelines for writing in these styles also apply to participating in a debate, giving a persuasive speech or giving an informative talk.

Read the following advice on argumentative and discursive writing. Then choose one of the questions that follow.

Argumentative writing

In an argumentative letter or article (or a persuasive speech) you take a particular point of view and argue the case, demonstrating why you think it is the best. To strengthen your argument, it is important to show that you have considered both sides of the argument. A balanced approach, giving the counter-arguments, is often a good way of highlighting the flaws in opposing points of view and adding credibility to your own. Plan your writing so that weak arguments and/or opposing views come first.

Discursive writing

A discursive letter or article is more informative: you discuss a range of possible views and then, if appropriate, outline your own thoughts on the subject.

Features of both styles

- You need a concise, effective introduction to capture the reader's attention and make the topic clear.

- Using personal pronouns *I*, *you* and *we* makes your writing more effective, but avoid getting too passionate or personal. This will make you sound over-emotional and subjective, and therefore less convincing.

- For argumentative or discursive writing in an exam, read, re-read and keyword the question carefully. There is often a single word in the question that affects the nature or emphasis of the argument. Underline words such as *obligatory*, *compulsory* or *always*.

- Think about the subject of the writing and plan carefully. Check the question and your plans as you go along to ensure your paragraphs have a logical structure and do not drift off the topic.

- Always give your writing a title.

- Never start paragraphs with *firstly, secondly, thirdly*. Use linking words that lead from one aspect of your argument to the next, for example: *furthermore*, *on the other hand*, *nevertheless*.

- Avoid using rhetorical questions and never end with a question such as: *So, what do you think?*

- Find an interesting, convincing way to close the writing. Avoid weak endings such as *to sum up* and *in conclusion*.

Write an article for a school magazine on teachers or the older generation as role models.

Choose one of the questions below and write in either a discursive or an argumentative style.

Use the discursive/argumentative planning outline on page 29 to help you plan your article before you write the final version. Plan each paragraph carefully. Construct your argument or set out your ideas in a logical sequence so each paragraph contains a clear topic sentence that leads to a conclusion. Give your article a title. Use separate sheets of paper if necessary.

a. "Teachers shouldn't try to be friends or role models." What are your views?

OR

b. It's natural and right that the older generation should tell young people what to do. Older people have the experience to know what is right and wrong.

....
....
....
....
....
....
....
....
....
....
....
....
....
....
....
....
....
....
....
....
....
....

PLAN
Title:
Introduction – explain exactly what you are going to discuss
Statement – say what you think or believe
Topic 1 – show both sides of the argument and give examples
Example 1
Example 2
Transition
Topic 2 – if necessary, examine another aspect of what people think and give examples
Example 1
Example 2
Transition
Topic 3 – demonstrate that your argument or analysis is valid
Final example – a concluding example that defeats your opponent's viewpoint or justifies your analysis
Conclusion

4 "All the world's a stage"

Exploring the writer's craft

In this passage from her autobiography *At the Source*, Welsh author and poet Gillian Clarke describes nature in terms of theatre or a film. Read the passage and answer the questions that follow.

Paragraph 1

Paragraph 2

Paragraph 3

A wildlife spectacle

A flashback to kites falling on flesh. They appear out of the blue, at first just one or two specks in the sky, then more, until they are soaring in from all points over the mountains. Two or three hundred red kites firing in the sun as they flex and turn, homing down to a farm near Rhayader in mid-Wales. There, in a small   5
field, fresh, raw meat is tipped from a trailer at the same hour every day. Diversification in agriculture has rarely been so imaginatively conceived. This is theatre.

Once the news is out, every kite in the mountain heartland of Wales knows it. The day in spring when I visit, a BBC camera team   10
is preparing to film. Iolo Williams, 'the bird man', here to present the programme, tells me it is very likely that our kites from seventy miles away in Ceredigion are among these visitors, and that kites come to the feeding site from as far away as Yorkshire. How do they know? Do they have mobile phones?   15

First come the crows, minesweepers clearing the ground for the great arrival. Then the buzzards, outriders taking the risk to get a first snatch at the feast. Once the crows and buzzards have retreated to the trees with their share of flesh, and the lie of the

land looks safe, the first kite appears, distantly floating on the 20
thermals above the mountains. According to the farm's website,
on rare occasions, during strange weather maybe, the crows and
the buzzards have failed to arrive to feed. On those days the kites
eye the ground from afar but come no closer. But today all is well.
Crow and buzzard descend and fly off, then singly, in twos, tens, 25
hundreds, the angelic host blazes down on a field of blood.

***

Now it is August, and here, over our fields, seventy miles
south-west of that spectacular daily event, kites are a common
sight these days. This scavenger of the streets of medieval London
was persecuted, shot by gamekeepers, its nests plundered by egg 30
collectors until it was Britain's rarest bird. A few birds survived
in its heartland in the mountains of mid-Wales, though at worst,
according to reports of studies using DNA evidence, its numbers
were reduced to the offspring of a single female.

The other day a huge combine harvester was at work in our 35
neighbour's big barley field. All day, as the monstrous machine
growled up and down the field, four kites haunted the sky, causing
consternation to the buzzards and a crowd of crows competing to
feed on fresh kill: crushed mice, voles, rabbits, frogs.

A kite is a parable of beauty and violence. Its obsession, its 40
golden eye burning the ground for blood, the unflinching instinct
to survive. Riding the thermals, it flexes its wings and long forked
tail in independent movements – the only bird which can do that –
flaunting its auburns, manoeuvring the wind. As it drops on injured
prey or carrion it scarcely touches the ground. Such lazy grace, 45
such beauty, such savagery!

A ewe died deep in the gorse last winter, too far inside the thicket
to be discovered except by foxes and crows. Gorse makes a fortified
city, arched, aisled and alley-wayed for fox and badger or an old
sheep seeking respite from wind and rain. The kite circled, waiting, 50
while the crows and the buzzards ripped open the carcase. Then
it descended in slow, elegant circles, fell on the body, and gorged.
Flamboyance – that's the word I want, flame on air – its reds all
the more fiery against the clean bow of white under the span of its
wings, the black bars on its tail. Beautiful, gorging, gorgeous. 55

Paragraph 4

Paragraph 5

Paragraph 6

Paragraph 7

Kite (n): a large bird of prey.

Minesweeper (n): ships used for clearing away explosive mines in the sea

Buzzard (n): a bird of prey.

1. Match each of the following headings to one of the paragraphs in the passage. One has been done for you.
   a. Warfare ....
   b. Background history ....
   c. Anecdote 1 ....
   d. Paradox ....
   e. Anecdote 2 ....
   f. Spectacle ....*1*...............

2. In your own words explain how and why the author uses the following words and expressions. Use a dictionary to help you.
   a. "A flashback" (line 1)

   ....

   ....

   b. "homing down to a farm" (lines 4–5)

   ....

   ....

   c. "This is theatre." (line 8)

   ....

   ....

   d. "the lie of the land looks safe" (lines 19–20)

   ....

   ....

   e. "causing consternation" (lines 37–8)

   ....

   ....

   f. "a crowd of crows" (line 38)

   ....

   ....

   g. "A kite is a parable of beauty and violence." (line 40)

   ....

   ....

   h. "a fortified city" (lines 48–9)

   ....

   ....

   i. "Flamboyance" (line 53)

   ....

   ....

   j. "Beautiful, gorging, gorgeous." (line 55)

   ....

   ....

3. Using your own words as far as possible, explain how and why the author uses the following literary features to describe birds in mid-Wales.

   a. Find two examples of metaphor and explain how they are used.

   ....

   ....

   ....

   b. Find two examples of paradox or oxymoron and explain the author's choice of words.

   ....

   ....

   ....

   c. Find two examples of alliteration and explain the effects.

   ....

   ....

   ....

   d. Find one example of visual imagery and explain the author's choice of words.

   ....

   ....

   ....

   e. Find one example of aural (or auditory) imagery and explain the author's choice of words.

   ....

   ....

   ....

Using English: proverbs and clichés

A proverb is a popular saying often expressed in a clever, brief way.

A cliché is an over-used expression that has been repeated so often it has lost its originality and in some cases its original meaning.

1. Read the following proverbs and explain what they mean in your own words.

   a. The early bird catches the worm.

   ....

   ....

   b. Absence makes the heart grow fonder.

   ....

   ....

   c. A stitch in time saves nine.

   ....

   ....

   d. Don't count your chickens until they're hatched.

   ....

   ....

   e. Empty vessels make the most noise.

   ....

   ....

2. Many proverbs have become so common that we only need to quote half or part of them for someone to understand what we are trying to say. Try to complete the following examples.

   a. There's no smoke ....

   b. A bird in the hand ....

   c. A friend in need ....

   d. Nothing ventured ....

   e. Too many cooks ....

3. Some popular expressions have become so over-used that they are now clichés. Using clichés in your writing shows a lack of imagination.

Find interesting, original ways to finish the following similes.

a. As good as ....

b. As black as ....

c. It'll spread like ....

d. These will sell like ....

e. He's as strong as ....

4. Tick the comparisons that, in your opinion, are now clichés.

a. Like a fish out of water ☐

b. Like a headless chicken ☐

c. Like greased lightning ☐

d. Like a bull in a china shop ☐

e. Like there's no tomorrow ☐

5. Find more interesting and imaginative ways to say each of the following examples.

a. Having a whale of a time

....

b. On cloud nine

....

c. Keeping a low profile

....

d. Out in the sticks

....

e. Lost to the world

....

5 Family and friends

Interpreting the meaning of new words

You may encounter words and phrases that are new to you in the passage below. Try to answer the questions that follow by looking at the context of the words. Do not use a dictionary or thesaurus to check your understanding of the words until you have completed the final question.

This first passage is from the autobiography of Mineko Iwasaki, a retired Japanese geisha. A geisha is a woman who has received rigorous training from childhood to sing and dance in the classical Japanese style. Mineko is explaining something of her father's family history.

Peerage: the nobility; high-ranking members of society.

Family history

Great changes took place in Japan in the middle of the nineteenth century. The military dictatorship that had ruled the country for 650 years was overthrown and Emperor Meiji was installed as the head of the government. The feudal system was dismantled and Japan began to develop into a modern nation state. Led by the Emperor, the aristocrats and intellectuals began a lively debate about the future of the country.

At that time, my great-grandfather, Tanakaminamoto no Sukeyoshi, was also ready for a change. He was tired of the endless factional infighting of the aristocracy and wanted to rid himself of the onerous duties his position demanded.

When the Emperor decided to move the Imperial Capital from Kyoto, where it had been for over a millennium, to Tokyo, he saw his chance. My family's roots ran deep in their home soil, and they didn't want to leave Kyoto. As head of the family, my great-grandfather made the momentous decision to give back his title and join the ranks of the commoners.

Emperor Meiji pressed him to remain in the peerage but he proudly declared that he was a man of the people. The Emperor insisted that he at least retain his name, which he agreed to do. In daily life the family now uses the shortened form of Tanaka.

Though noble in sentiment, my great-grandfather's decision was disastrous for the family's finances. Giving up his title, of course, 30 meant forfeiting the property that went along with it. The family's estates had covered a vast area of north-eastern Kyoto, from Tanaka Shrine in the south to Ichijoji Temple in the north, an 35 area thousands of acres in size.

My great-grandfather and his descendants never recovered from the loss. They were unable to gain a foothold in the modern economy that was propelling the country, and languished in genteel 40 poverty, living off their savings and thriving on their outmoded sense of inherent superiority.

From *The Geisha of Gion*, by Mineko Iwasaki

1. Rewrite the following quotations in your own words (given the context of the passage). Use a dictionary to help you.

   a. "The military dictatorship that had ruled the country for 650 years was overthrown" (lines 2–4)

   ....

   ....

   b. "The feudal system was dismantled" (lines 5–6)

   ....

   ....

   c. "the endless factional infighting of the aristocracy" (lines 12–13)

   ....

   ....

   d. "the onerous duties his position demanded" (line 14)

   ....

   ....

   e. a "momentous decision" (line 21)

   ....

   ....

   f. "forfeiting the property" (line 32)

   ....

   ....

   g. "genteel poverty" (lines 40–1)

   ....

   ....

Now read the next passage in which Mineko Iwasaki explains something of her mother's family history and describes how her parents met. Then answer the question that follows.

Family history

My mother Chie is a member of the Akamatsu family. In olden times, they were legendary pirates who buccaneered the trade routes around the Inland Sea and out towards Korea and China, amassing a fortune in ill-gotten gains that they managed to transform into legitimate wealth by the time my mother came along. The Akamatsu family never served any *Daimyo* (military governor), but themselves had the power and property to govern Western Japan. The family was awarded the name Akamatsu by Emperor Gotoba (1180–1239).

While adventuring in 'foreign commodities' the family gained much knowledge about medicinal herbs and their preparation. They studied the art of healing and eventually rose to become house physicians to the Ikeda clan, the feudal barons of Okayama. My mother inherited these skills from her ancestors and passed her knowledge on to my father.

My parents were both artists. My father graduated from art school and became a professional painter of textiles for high quality kimono and an appraiser of fine porcelain.

My mother loved kimono. One day, while visiting a kimono shop, she happened to run into my father, who fell in love with her on the spot. He pursued her quite relentlessly. Their class differences were such that my mother felt a relationship was impossible. [...]

At the time my father was very successful and making a lot of money. His creations attracted the highest prices and he was bringing home a good income every month. But he was giving most of this to his parents, who had little other source of funds. My grandparents lived with their extended family in an enormous home in the Tanaka section of town that was manned by a large staff of servants. By the 1930s the family had gone through most of its savings. Some of the men had tried their hand at civil servant work, but nobody was able to hold on to a job for very long. They simply had no tradition of working for a living. My father was supporting the entire household.

So, even though my father wasn't the oldest son, my grandparents insisted that he and my mother live with them when they got married. Basically, they needed the money.

It was not a happy situation. My grandmother, whose name was Tamiko, was an overbearingly flamboyant character, both autocratic and short-tempered, the exact opposite of my gentle, docile mother. My mother was the one who had been raised like a princess, but my grandmother treated her just like a servant. She was abusive to her from the start and berated her constantly for her common background. There were some notorious criminals within the Akamatsu lineage and my grandmother acted as if my mother was polluted. She didn't think the young woman was nearly good enough for her son.

Grandmother Tamiko's hobby was fencing, and she was a master at wielding the *naginata*, or Japanese halberd. My mother's docility drove the older woman crazy and she started to taunt her by threatening her openly with the curved lance of her weapon. She'd even chase her around the house! It was bizarre and frightening. On one occasion, my grandmother went too far. She repeatedly slashed through my mother's *obi* (kimono sash), severing it from her body. That was the final straw.

From *The Geisha of Gion*, by Mineko Iwasaki

> **Appraiser:** a valuer, who judges the quality of something and may set its price.

2. Imagine you are either Mineko's mother or her father. Write an entry in your diary for what happened on the day Grandmother Tamiko slashed through Chie's kimono sash with her sword. Include the following:

- what happened
- why Grandmother Tamiko was using a sword
- why Grandmother Tamiko bullied Chie
- what you think about Grandmother Tamiko's behaviour.

Write between 250 and 350 words.

Reminder

In this type of empathic question you are being asked to analyse, evaluate and develop material from the text. When a question starts with "You are …" or "Imagine you are …", re-read the passage from that person's point of view and then express what that person thinks, feels and/or imagines.

....
....
....
....
....
....
....
....
....
....
....
....
....
....
....
....
....
....
....
....
....

Using English: irregular verbs

In each of the sentences below there are two words in brackets. One is grammatically correct; the other may be something we say, but is technically incorrect. Circle the correct option in each case.

a. After he had (run, ran) about a kilometer, he (sank, sunk) to his knees with exhaustion.

b. Cloth is (wove, woven) from a type of wool that has (grown, grew) on local sheep.

c. The timid deer was (drove, driven) into a narrow valley where it was (slew, slain) by a tiger.

d. A tree had (fell, fallen) during a storm; its branches lay (broke, broken) all around it.

e. The sketch had been (drew, drawn) by a famous painter whose name was (wrote, written) at the bottom of the picture.

Using a dictionary or thesaurus

Read the passage below, then answer the questions that follow.

In the late 16th and early 17th centuries, people from the British Isles were taking their already hybrid language to the New World and other lands across the sea, expanding their vocabulary to suit new experiences. However, something else was happening to the words in the English language within the British Isles. The invention of printing and the immediate popularity of printed books meant the different forms of English spoken in the British Isles needed to be standardised. As books became cheaper and more people learned to read, spelling and grammar became more (but not entirely) fixed, and the dialect of London, where most publishing houses were set up, became Standard English.

The first English dictionary was published in 1604. It was called *A Table Alphabeticall* and was written by a schoolteacher named Robert Cawdray. Then came a series of dictionaries that explained, in a simplified form, strange and difficult words. For example, the *New World of English Words* by Edward Phillips was published in 1658 and dealt with difficult and technical terms mostly taken from earlier dictionaries.

The meaning of the word *thesaurus* is from the Greek *thēsauros* for storehouse or treasure. The original sense of a thesaurus as a dictionary or encyclopaedia of words was narrowed down to being a list of selected words, concepts and synonyms by the publication of Roget's *Thesaurus of English Words and Phrases* in 1852. Roget's classification system took nearly 50 years to perfect and his thesaurus was not published until he was 73 years old. Only 1000 copies of the first edition were printed. The original structure has changed little since 1852, although it now includes many scientific and technological words. Today, Roget's *Thesaurus of English Words and Phrases* is one of the most used reference books in the world.

There are now two main kinds of thesaurus: a Roget-type with a category system and an A-to-Z thesaurus that looks more like a dictionary. If you are using a Roget-type thesaurus, become familiar with the way words are organised. To find a word, you need to go to the index first. The index will tell you which words are nouns, verbs and adjectives and give you a number. You then look for that number in the main body of the thesaurus.

It is a good idea to look at alternative words to use in your writing and not limit yourself to the ones you think you know. However, take care not to use an interesting new word that doesn't fit the context of your sentence. An A-to-Z thesaurus will help you because it gives you definitions, but you still need to take care to use an appropriate word for the context.

Hybrid: something created by combining different elements, species or varieties.

1. Look at these alternatives for the verb *speak*.

inform	mention	tell	say	utter	mutter
pronounce	blurt out	declare	divulge	chatter	gossip

   a. Which of the verbs in the box fits in this sentence?

   He planned to speak to her the minute he got home; he would .... *her the good news immediately.*

   b. Is there a synonym below that you could use instead? If not, why not?

inform	intimate	apprise	acquaint
instruct	mention	state	reveal

2. Write a sentence to show the meaning of each of the following verbs and phrasal verbs. They can all be used to replace *to see* or *look at*.

   a. glance

   ....

   b. catch a glimpse of

   ....

   c. peer

   ....

   d. gaze

   ....

   e. observe

   ....

   f. peep

   ....

   g. distinguish

   ....

   h. catch sight of

   ....

   i. detect

   ....

   j. locate

   ....

3. The English language has a rich and wide vocabulary because it uses words from different origins. In choosing verbs, for example, we can say we *listened* to the radio and *heard* the news or we *watched* a football match and *saw* the winning goal.

   Read the following passage about how we communicate and how people respond when we speak to them. Choose the appropriate verb from the box to fill each gap, using the correct tense (past/present/ future). You can use the same verb more than once. Two examples have been done for you.

| to ask | to speak | to inform | to tell | to request | to respond | to answer |
| to talk | to discuss | to chat | to reply | | | |

Dutch is **(a)** *spoken* as the native language throughout the Netherlands, but many people also **(b)** *speak* English and other languages. The Dutch seem to have a natural ability for foreign tongues. Unfortunately I don't, and I certainly can't **(c)** .... a word of Dutch. When my train stopped in the Hague I had to **(d)** .... a porter at the station if he could tell me the way to the main shopping street in English. He **(e)** .... in English, but he **(f)** .... with such a curious intonation I didn't understand much of what he **(g)** .... I tried again in my bad school French, but he obviously couldn't understand what I was **(h)** .... so I looked around for someone else to **(i)** .... and found a policeman who **(j)** .... excellent English and seemed pleased to have an opportunity to **(k)** .... to someone. We **(l)** .... about this and that for some minutes. However by the time I had managed to get away from the station (and the policeman) I had forgotten what I had been **(m)** .... I did eventually find the main shopping street, but to **(n)** .... the truth, I'm not sure how I got there.

Using English: splitting infinitives

The infinitive is usually two words as in *to read* or *to write*, but we sometimes contract these two words to one. For example:

•   *I helped **pack** her bag.* (I helped her **to pack** her bag.)

You may have heard of the grammatical offence of splitting the infinitive.

•   *I helped her **to** <u>quickly</u> **pack** her bag.* ✗

•   *I helped her **to pack** her bag <u>quickly</u>.* ✔

Splitting the infinitive means separating the two words of an infinitive (*to* + verb) by putting an adverb or other words between them. For example:

•   *I can't claim **to** <u>completely and honestly</u> **understand** this explanation.* ✗

We often split infinitives when we are speaking, but it is incorrect and looks clumsy in writing so it should be avoided.

Identify the split infinitives in these sentences and rewrite each sentence correctly.

a. Ask Mrs Adams to briefly explain what she wants us to do for homework.

....

b. Do you promise to obediently and loyally follow your leader?

....

c. He tried to eloquently express his true emotions, but she laughed at him.

....

d. I am writing to humbly apologise for hurting your feelings.

....

e. Try to clearly and accurately describe what you see.

....

Using English: sinister words

Here is part of a project on the way the English language uses words related to left-handedness by a student named Jamie, who is the heroine of the novel *On the Other Hand* by Jean Gill.

Left-handers unite!

The English language is prejudiced against left-handers. The word 'left' is from the Saxon word 'lyft', which had two meanings: 'left' and 'useless'.

It is not all left to make someone else feel inferior – ban these words!

Word	Meaning	
maladroit	clumsy	(from the French for 'bad on the right')
gauche	clumsy	(from the French for 'left')
sinister	wicked	(from the Latin for 'left')
awkward	clumsy	(from the Middle English 'awke' meaning 'from the left')
gawky	unco-ordinated	(meaning 'from the left')
adroit	deft	(clever with hands from the French for 'right')
dexterous	good with hands	(from the Latin for 'right')
ambidextrous	good with both hands	(from the Latin for having two right hands)
righteous	good	
right	straight, correct, not left	(from the Latin for straight, right (side))
to have two left feet	to be clumsy	

IS IT ANY WONDER WE LEFT-HANDERS FEEL CLUMSY?!!

What did the Romans ever do for us?

The Romans invented the right-handed handshake as a way of showing you were not carrying a weapon … but if you were left-handed, you could shake hands right-handed AND stab someone with the dagger in your left hand – SINISTER!

The Romans gave us our alphabet, which reads from left to right –

COULD THAT BE WHY MORE LEFT-HANDERS ARE DYSLEXIC?

?dednah-tfel uoy erA	?ylisae siht daer uoy naC
?ylisae erom siht daer uoy naC	.gnitirwdnah tfel-ot-thgir ni seiraid sih etorw icniVad odranoeL

Using Jamie's project to help you, find the answers to the clues below in the word search. Some of the words go from left to right, but a few are more tricky.

a	e	q	t	n	i	p	h	a	s	f	b
w	m	a	l	a	d	r	o	i	t	r	g
k	p	b	y	c	z	b	m	k	u	f	a
w	m	s	i	n	i	s	t	e	r	h	u
a	t	n	u	d	o	i	s	v	m	k	c
r	i	g	h	t	e	o	u	s	o	e	h
d	w	t	k	m	v	x	w	z	o	p	e
o	a	a	d	r	z	i	t	e	g	n	k
h	p	r	g	j	e	o	p	r	n	r	t
t	w	m	o	d	t	j	a	s	o	a	i
k	a	r	d	e	x	t	e	r	o	u	s
m	y	a	k	b	e	i	d	m	j	o	s

Clues

- clumsy 1
- clumsy 2
- clumsy 3
- deft
- good
- good with both hands
- good with hands
- involving wickedness

Practising reading comprehension

Read this passage and answer the questions that follow on a separate sheet of paper.

The Phoenix

Lord Strawberry, a nobleman, collected birds. He had the finest aviary in Europe, so large that eagles did not find it uncomfortable, so well laid out that both humming birds and snow-buntings had a climate that suited them perfectly. But for many years the finest set of apartments remained empty, with just a label saying: "PHOENIX. Habitat: Arabia." 5

Many authorities on bird life had assured Lord Strawberry that the phoenix is a fabulous bird, or that the breed was long extinct. Lord Strawberry was unconvinced: his family had always believed in phoenixes. At intervals he received from his agents (together with statements of their expenses) birds which they declared were the phoenix but which turned out to be orioles, macaws, turkey buzzards dyed orange, etc., or stuffed cross-breeds, ingeniously assembled from various plumages. Finally Lord Strawberry went himself to Arabia, where, after some months, he 10 15 20 found a phoenix, won its confidence, caught it, and brought it home in perfect condition.

It was a remarkably fine phoenix, with a charming character – affable to the other birds in the aviary and much attached to Lord Strawberry. 25 On its arrival in England it made a greatest stir among ornithologists, journalists, poets, and milliners, and was constantly visited. But it was not puffed by these attentions, and when it was no longer in the news, and the visits fell off, it 30 showed no pique or rancour. It ate well, and seemed perfectly contented.

It costs a great deal of money to keep up an aviary. When Lord Strawberry died he died penniless. The aviary came on the market. In 35 normal times the rarer birds, and certainly the phoenix, would have been bid for by the trustees of Europe's great zoological societies, or by private persons in the U.S.A.; but as it happened Lord Strawberry died just after a world war, when 40 both money and bird-seed were hard to come by (indeed the cost of bird-seed was one of the things which had ruined Lord Strawberry). The London *Times* urged in a leader that the phoenix be bought for the London Zoo, saying that a nation 45 of bird-lovers had a moral right to own such a rarity; and a fund, called the Strawberry Phoenix Fund, was opened. Students, naturalists, and school-children contributed according to their means; but their means were small, and there 50 were no large donations. So Lord Strawberry's executors (who had the death duties to consider) closed with the higher offer of Mr. Tancred Poldero, owner and proprietor of Poldero's Wizard Wonderworld. 55

For quite a while Mr. Poldero considered his phoenix a bargain. It was a civil and obliging bird, and adapted itself readily to its new surroundings. It did not cost much to feed, it did not mind children; and though it had no tricks, Mr. Poldero 60 supposed it would soon pick up some. The publicity of the Strawberry Phoenix Fund was now most helpful. Almost every contributor now saved up another half-crown in order to see the phoenix. Others, who had not contributed to the fund, even 65 paid double to look at it on the five-shilling days.

But then business slackened. The phoenix was as handsome as ever, and amiable; but, as Mr. Poldero said, it hadn't got Udge. Even at popular prices the phoenix was not really popular. 70 It was too quiet, too classical. So people went instead to watch the antics of the baboons, or to admire the crocodile who had eaten the woman.

One day Mr. Poldero said to his manager, Mr. Ramkin: 75

"How long since any fool paid to look at the phoenix?"

"Matter of three weeks," replied Mr. Ramkin.

"Eating his head off," said Mr. Poldero. "Let alone the insurance. Seven shillings a week it 80 costs me to insure the Archbishop of Canterbury."

"The public don't like him. He's too quiet for them, that's the trouble. Won't mate nor nothing. And I've tried him with no end of pretty pollies, ospreys, and Cochin-Chinas, and the Lord knows 85 what. But he won't look at them."

"Wonder if we could swap him for a livelier one," said Mr. Poldero.

"Impossible. There's only one of him at a time."

"Go on!" 90

"I mean it. Haven't you ever read what it says on the label?"

They went to the phoenix's cage. It flapped its wings politely, but they paid no attention. They read:

"PANSY. *Phoenix phoenixissima formossisima* 95 *arabiana*. This rare and fabulous bird is unique. The World's Old Bachelor. Has no mate and doesn't want one. When old, sets fire to itself and emerges miraculously reborn. Specially imported from the East." 100

"I've got an idea," said Mr. Poldero. "How old do you suppose that bird is?"

"Looks in its prime to me," said Mr. Ramkin.

"Suppose," continued Mr. Poldero, "we could somehow get him alight? We'd advertise it 105 beforehand, of course, work up interest. Then we'd have a new bird, and a bird with some romance about it, a bird with a life story. We could sell a bird like that."

Mr. Ramkin nodded. 110

"I've read about it in a book," he said. "You've got to give them scented woods and what not, and they build a nest and sit down on it and catch fire spontaneous. But they won't do it till they're old. That's the snag." 115

"Leave that to me," said Mr. Poldero. "You get those scented woods, and I'll do the ageing."

It was not easy to age the phoenix. Its allowance of food was halved, and halved again, but though it grew thinner its eyes were undimmed and its 120 plumage glossy as ever. The heating was turned off; but it puffed out its feathers against the cold, and seemed none the worse. Other birds were put into its cage, birds of a peevish and quarrelsome nature. They pecked and chivvied it; but the 125 phoenix was so civil and amiable that after a day or two they lost their animosity. Then Mr. Poldero tried alley cats. These could not be won by manners, but the phoenix darted above their heads and flapped its golden wings in their faces, and daunted them.

Mr. Poldero turned to a book on Arabia, and read that the climate was dry. "Aha!" said he. The phoenix was moved to a small cage that had a sprinkler in the ceiling. Every night the sprinkler was turned on. The phoenix began to cough. Mr. Poldero had another good idea. Daily he stationed himself in front of the cage to jeer at the bird and abuse it.

When spring was come, Mr. Poldero felt justified in beginning a publicity campaign about the ageing phoenix. The old public favourite, he said, was nearing its end. Meanwhile he tested the bird's reactions every few days by putting a few tufts of foul-smelling straw and some strands of rusty barbed wire into the cage, to see if it were interested in nesting yet. One day the phoenix began turning over the straw. Mr. Poldero signed a contract for the film rights. At last the hour seemed ripe. It was a fine Saturday evening in May. For some weeks the public interest in the ageing phoenix had been working up, and the admission charge had risen to five shillings. The enclosure was thronged. The lights and the cameras were trained on the cage, and a loud-speaker proclaimed to the audience the rarity of what was about to take place.

"The phoenix," said the loud-speaker, "is the aristocrat of bird-life. Only the rarest and most expensive specimens of oriental wood, drenched in exotic perfumes, will tempt him to construct his strange love-nest."

Now a neat assortment of twigs and shavings, strongly scented, was shoved into the cage.

"The phoenix," the loud-speaker continued, "is as capricious as Cleopatra, as luxurious as la du Barry, as heady as a strain of wild gypsy music. All the fantastic pomp and passion of the ancient East, its languorous magic, its subtle cruelties . . ."

"Lawks!" cried a woman in the crowd. "He's at it!"

A quiver stirred the dulled plumage. The phoenix turned its head from side to side. It descended, staggering, from its perch. Then wearily it began to pull about the twigs and shavings.

The cameras clicked, the lights blazed full on the cage. Rushing to the loud-speaker Mr. Poldero exclaimed:

"Ladies and gentlemen, this is the thrilling moment the world has breathlessly awaited. The legend of centuries is materializing before our modern eyes. The phoenix …"

The phoenix settled on its pyre and appeared to fall asleep.

The film director said:

"Well, if it doesn't evaluate more than this, mark instructional."

At that moment the phoenix and the pyre burst into flames. The flames streamed upwards, leaped out on every side. In a minute or two everything was burned to ashes, and some thousand people, including Mr. Poldero, perished in the blaze.

by Silvia Townsend Warner

Milliners people who make women's hats.

Leader leading article in a newspaper.

Half-crown a coin worth two shillings and sixpence in old British money (a considerable amount in those days).

Archbishop of Canterbury Poldero is referring to the phoenix and its quiet respectability.

1. Answer the following questions in full sentences.

    a. Why did Lord Strawberry want the phoenix? (1 mark)

    b. Describe the conditions in Lord Strawberry's aviary. (1 mark)

    c. Why does Poldero acquire the phoenix? (1 mark)

    d. How does Poldero keep the phoenix at his Wizard Wonderland to begin with? (1 mark)

    e. What do you think Poldero means by "(the phoenix) hadn't got Udge" (line 69)? (2 marks)

    f. In your opinion, why did people lose interest in the phoenix and go to see the crocodile instead? (2 marks)

    g. Why does Poldero decide to 'age' the phoenix? (2 marks)

    h. Describe how Poldero encourages the phoenix to die. (3 marks)

    i. Explain when and why Poldero begins a publicity campaign. (2 marks)

    j. What happens to the people who came to witness the phoenix die? (2 marks)

    k. Why do you think the author ended her story in this way? (3 marks)

2. Re-read the different ways the phoenix is described at the beginning and end of the story. Examine:

    a. what the narrator says about the bird when it is acquired for Poldero's Wizard Wonderland

    b. what the loud-speaker says about the phoenix when the press and public come to see it die.

    Select words and phrases from these descriptions to show how the writer makes the reader feel sorry for the bird. (5 marks)

                                                            (25 marks)

Using English: new words for new inventions

1. New words have to be invented to name and describe new inventions or social developments.

   Write a few words about how and why each of the following words came into use. The first one has been done for you.

   a. Steamship

   Before steam ships were invented big ships had sails and were called sailing ships. Steamships were propelled using coal to make steam, like steam trains.

   b. Telegraph

   ....

   ....

   ....

   c. Railroad

   ....

   ....

   ....

   d. Department store

   ....

   ....

   ....

   e. Package tour

   ....

   ....

   ....

   f. Space shuttle

   ....

   ....

   ....

2. The automobile was so called because it was self-propelled (*auto + mobile*). Since the invention of the automobile, names have been carefully selected to suggest the qualities of each new vehicle and appeal to a particular type of buyer.

   Write a few words to say what the names of each of these Ford models suggests to you.

   a. Popular

   ....

   ....

   ....

   b. Ranch Wagon

   ....

   ....

   ....

   c. Fiesta

   ....

   ....

   ....

   d. Transit

   ....

   ....

   ....

   e. Thunderbird

   ....

   ....

   ....

Using English: relative clauses

A **defining relative clause** gives essential information about the noun or noun phrase it modifies, in order to identify exactly who or what is being referred to. Removing the information in this clause would result in the sentence having a different meaning or no meaning at all. For example:

- The boy who stole my watch lives in my street.

If you remove the clause "who stole my watch", the sentence reads:

- The boy lives in my street.

There are many boys living in your street. Which boy are you talking about?

1. Delete the defining relative clause from the following two sentences.

   a. The hotel that we stayed in on our school trip to London was very big.

   b. The guide who showed us round the Tower of London was very funny.

   As you can see, the phrase "that we stayed in on our school trip to London" tells you which hotel is being referred to. There are thousands of hotels in London, so it defines the exact hotel.

   There may be many amusing tour guides in London, but the phrase "who showed us round the Tower of London" identifies that we are referring to the one working in the Tower of London.

Non-defining relative clauses provide additional information that is not essential to understanding the meaning of the sentence. For example:

- My best friend Terry, who keeps white mice, lives next door to us.

"My best friend Terry lives next door to us" provides a valid piece of information. The fact that he keeps white mice is interesting, but not essential to understanding where Terry lives. The information between commas about the white mice is a non-defining relative clause.

2. Delete the non-defining relative clauses from these sentences.

   a. The book we're studying this term, which I've read before, is called *Lord of the Flies*.

   b. *Lord of the Flies* tells the story of a group of boys who crash land on an island, while being evacuated during a war, and how they survive without adults.

   c. George Orwell, who lived in what used to be called Burma when he was young, is famous for writing *Animal Farm* and *1984*.

   d. *Animal Farm*, whose real hero is a carthorse called Boxer, is an allegory of the Russian Revolution.

   e. The character of Boxer, who is very hardworking, represents Russian labourers.

> **Reminder**
>
> - *Who*, *whom*, *whose* and *that* are used for defining people.
>
> - *Which*, *whose* and *that* are used for things.
>
> - Defining relative clauses do not need commas.

As you can see, the non-defining relative clauses add extra information that is useful or interesting but not essential to the sentence.

3. Decide whether each of the following sentences contains a defining or a non-defining relative clause. The first one has been done for you.

		Defining	Non-defining
a.	Marianne, who always comes top in tests, is the only girl I know who plays a trumpet.		✔
b.	Paula can't go on the trip because her twin brother Joey, whose name is really Joshua, has broken his leg and she's got to stay at home to help look after him.		
c.	Money that had been stolen from our school safe was found in a classroom.		
d.	Jack's mother, who can play the violin, makes delicious cakes for our school tuck shop.		
e.	Jack's mother's violin, which she'll be playing at our school charity concert, is extremely valuable.		

4. Write a short paragraph of more than two sentences about a book you have read recently. Vary your sentences so they contain defining and non-defining relative clauses.

....

....

....

....

....

....

....

....

....

Practising directed writing

Read this verbatim interview with the Spanish founder of a charity named *Anidan* and then do the Directed Writing task that follows.

Anidan is an NGO [non-government organization], founded by Rafael Selas, to care for the needs of young children in Kenya. On the island of Lamu, off the northern coast, he has a Shelter where he houses 100 children but feeds, dresses, cares for and educates over 200.

Rafael Selas worked in Miami as a record producer for Sky before travelling to Africa and deciding to help the neediest kids in Lamu.

You founded Anidan in 2002. Could you give us your thoughts on the evolution of Anidan since its creation?

I founded Asociación Anidan in Madrid and Anidan Kenya with Nairobi's NGO Board seven years ago, with the aim to deliver quality help, hope and happiness to the neediest kids in Lamu that I met during two summer vacations. Once I had experienced the tough reality in Lamu I felt hope was the most important thing to bring here, as well as good examples and competitive projects. Then some papers about the situation of the orphans here by UNICEF [United Nations Children's Fund] made me realize that I couldn't abandon them. After all, leaving someone behind may be the worst for these kids. At Anidan they value most of all finding food, love and education, as well as a caring, big family that fights for them daily.

My first steps were helping the local orphanage with my savings, but soon I came to realize that unless I had my own organization I would never achieve complete satisfaction with the outcome of my aid. After using up all my savings on a pilot phase with a dozen kids, and once the project was showing success, we started getting most finance from Anidan's members, mostly people close to me. [...] Soon we were helping over fifty kids living in extremely difficult situations.

To offer kids on the streets a way out [of poverty] and into society was a big challenge so I got involved in establishing a fully Kenyan organization and team of staff to attend the kids and shelter those in most need. All thanks to the support from friends and family who have helped me from the very beginning. [...]

Could you give us some key figures of Anidan?

Currently we offer shelter, food, education, health and basic needs to around 240 kids on a daily basis; about half of them are living in our dorms. Last year we opened a free hospital for children in memory of Pablo Horstmann, thanks to the support of his foundation (Fundación Pablo Horstmann). We expect to attend to about 20,000 children from the region this year and fight back the high infant death rate. [...] In Madrid we have up to 20 volunteers who help with Asociación Anidan's work so money raised reaches Lamu and is used directly on our children. In Kenya we count on 60 employees, 59 are Kenyans [...] We also help them to study and grow professionally, thus safeguarding the future of the project.

The hospital was inaugurated in March 2008. How is this helping to reduce child mortality rate in the area?

By bringing free quality medical assistance to an area where the majority would not have access to such services and kids die for all kinds of reasons, from malaria, diarrhoea, AIDS, pneumonia, undernourishment. [...] Infant mortality was as high as 12% in Amu District. Our goal is to bring it to less than 2% in the next two years. [...] It is a great luxury in a remote rural area to come across the work of our three doctors at Anidan who are so motivated to cope, in a place where Medical Officers have to face such an enormous task due to lack of physicians. There is a paediatrician from Spain, our head doctor, Loise Lalu, with great experience in Africa and lastly a Kenyan physician. There are also four nurses, two lab technicians and the whole of Anidan's team, everyone is learning much from that experience of sharing time and knowledge with international volunteers. For us offering free quality services goes hand in hand with knowledge transfer and we are making an effort to receive second opinions from doctors around the world via the Internet. […]

Private donations are essential to accomplish Anidan's vision. What message would you send to private donors interested in contributing financially?

75 Let us join at Anidan to fight poverty amongst infants in all its forms, to create hope for people who live in extreme need. Let us spread love and trust, so that future generations may get a chance. Any monthly amount makes all the difference; it'll translate into much help and happiness for needy 80 kids and mums. 85

90

Read the interview with Rafael Selas carefully and write a short informative article about his work with Anidan for your school magazine.

Write between 250 and 350 words. Use a separate sheet of paper if necessary.

- your opinion of what Anidan is doing in Lamu
- your views on whether your school could or should help
- ideas about how your school could help (if appropriate).

....

....

....

....

....

....

....

....

....

....

....

....

....

....

....

....

....

....

7 "Believe it or not"

Improving Directed Writing: news reports and articles

The purpose of news reports, whether it is online or in a printed newspaper, is to inform. News reports are shorter than magazine or newspaper articles and convey information as briefly as possible.

News reports use short paragraphs and combine details as succinctly and effectively as possible. For example:

> Pensioner Tom Wood was trapped for ten hours in a tree during a 50km-hour mini-hurricane while rescuing his neighbour's prize-winning cat.

A longer account of the event might read:

> Mr Thomas Wood, a retired railway engineer from north London with a serious heart condition, was forced to cling to the wildly swaying branch of a tree for ten hours last Thursday as strong winds gusting at a wind speed of 50 kph cut across southern England, destroying hedges and fences. His neighbour's cat, a prize-winning Persian Pink by the name of Little Missy Rose had climbed …

Read the following news report on an earthquake in Mexico and answer the question that follows.

Earthquake 7.6 magnitude shakes Mexico

By Juana Redondo

Major earthquake strikes south-western Mexico, frightening residents and shaking buildings. Local authorities say as yet there are no reported fatalities.

The US Geological Survey marked the quake at 7.6 on the Richter scale and located the epicentre in Guerrero state, near the Pacific Coast resort of Acapulco. 5

Mexican reports put the strength lower and Acapulco residents informed Reuters the quake was not as violent as others experienced in recent past. 10

The Pacific Tsunami Warning Centre said the inland earthquake would not generate a widespread tsunami but there was the possibility of after-shocks. 15

The quake was felt strongly in Mexico City where buildings shook and office employees fled into the street. Witnesses say traffic came to a standstill on roads leading out of the city centre as many people tried to flee the built-up areas. 20

"I thought my office block was going to collapse," said Esteban Garcia, 53, a businessman from a neighbourhood hit hard in the devastating 1985 earthquake, which killed thousands. "But we've lived through worse," he added with a smile. 25

The quake was felt as far away as Guatemala City. Local television reported some damage to roads, and electricity lines were down, but as yet no fatalities have been reported. 30

You are a journalist visiting the area at the time of the quake. Write a short article for your newspaper's weekend magazine describing your experience. Base your account on the information in this report and add details about your personal experience and feelings at the time.

Write between 250 and 350 words. Use a separate sheet of paper if necessary.

....
....
....
....
....
....
....
....
....
....
....
....
....

Using English: adjectives and adjectival phrases

An adjective describes a noun. An adjectival phrase is a group of words that together describe a noun or pronoun in a sentence, thus functioning as an adjective.

A single adjective usually goes before the noun: *an **expensive** meal, a **huge** diamond*.

An adjectival phrase usually goes after the noun. For example:

- The meal was **expensive but delicious**.
- The diamond was **huge and obviously very expensive**.

As you can see, an adjectival phrase can contain words that are not adjectives, such as *and/but* (connectives) or *obviously* (adverb).

1. In each sentence identify the noun and the adjectival phrase. The first one has been done for you below. Use red to underline the noun and yellow for the adjectival phrase.

   a. My holiday was wonderfully relaxing.

   b. The weather during the week was blissfully warm.

   c. We used the hotel swimming pool every day; it was heated and decorated with shells.

   d. My father caught a shark while he was fishing; it was quite small but had a huge mouth and needle-sharp teeth.

   noun

   adjectival phrase

2. Rewrite each sentence below to include extra information by using the words in brackets to make adjectival phrases. The first one has been done for you.

   a. The warrior wore a steel helmet. (shiny/lightweight)

   The warrior wore a helmet made of shiny lightweight steel.

   b. Everyone in the village was suffering from the effects of a drought. (devastating/year-long)

   ....

   ....

   c. They live in an old house. (dilapidated/16th-century/in need of repair)

   ....

   ....

   d. There is a Chinese vase on the table. (priceless/antique/finely decorated/Ming)

   ....

   ....

e. His action in the face of great danger resulted in a medal for bravery. (completely selfless/heroic)

....

....

3. Write three sentences containing adjectival phrases about one of the following:

- a concert
- a rescue
- a famous sportsman and/or sports event.

....

....

....

....

....

....

....

....

....

....

....

....

....

....

....

....

....

....

....

....

....

....

....

....

....

....

Exploring where poems come from

In the following two passages two poets, James Reeves and Gillian Clarke, discuss how poems are formed. Read both passages and answer the questions that follow.

Passage A: Where do poems come from?

If a poem is not simply printed words on a page, or a notation for a series of spoken sounds, what is it? It is most helpful at this point, I think, to regard a poem as an event. At best, it is a magical event; and at worst it is only the feeble shadow 5 of an event, or, if you like, an event that doesn't happen. […] The poem doesn't simply describe or relate an event in the poet's mind; it is itself an event. It doesn't happen in the poet's mind or anywhere else until it is written down, or at any 10 rate composed in the poet's mind. Nobody can generalize about the way in which every poet writes. But I think it is true to say that usually some sort of disturbance happens in the poet's mind, and this takes shape as an event which can 15 be communicated to others through the medium of the written word. A thunderstorm is an event which takes place in the atmosphere as the result of an electrical disturbance. Electric charges build up in the atmosphere until their force is released 20 as lightning and thunder. A poem can occur when some sort of force or pressure builds up in the poet's mind and demands release in the form of a poetic event. Its appearance need not be sudden or explosive like a thunderclap; it may be slow and 25 gradual. Nor, I must add, does this describe all kinds of poem; but I think it describes many of the best.

Until the poem has formed itself in the poet's mind – and it is unlikely to form itself completely except during the actual process of composition – 30 the poet cannot be absolutely certain what he is going to write. Once it has been discharged from his mind, it takes its place in the series of events which go to make up the sum of all poetry. The reader to whose consciousness the new event is 35 communicated will not get from the poem exactly the experience that built up in the poet's mind before he wrote it. But if the poem is a good one – or, put it in another way, if the event is charged with magic – he and countless other readers can 40 receive from it a shock or surprise. This is the shock of having a new experience. The reader's experience has been permanently enlarged.

From *Understanding Poetry* by James Reeves

Passage B: Where do poems come from?

Where do poems come from? An architect sees an interior before he sees the building. Before a roof and walls there is space and light. That's how it feels when a poem is about to form: there is an idea, an image, a fuzzy line, a fizzing excitement, 5 but the words have yet to speak. Even if there are words it is somehow too dark to read them, though a phrase or a line may be legible already. But as soon as this unclear vision declares its presence one can be certain that the poem can be written. 10

For me, the poem arrives in a coinciding moment of language and energy. Its subject is like a novelist's plot – merely an excuse to rummage in the mind for language. There are few plots and all writers share the same small store, using them 15 over and over again. When a poem is on the way it feels as though energy has been lying in wait for language. Or is it the other way about? And whence does that language come flooding, as strongly as any of the driving human passions, and as suddenly, 20 as mysteriously? The poem is begun in that moment of germination, though it must be unmade and made again in the cold light of the mind before it can be called a finished work of art. To have an *idea* for a poem is to have nothing at all. 25

From *At the Source* by Gillian Clarke

1. James Reeves likens a finished poem to an "event". Re-read lines 14–17 and explain in your own words what you think he means by "some sort of disturbance happens in the poet's mind, and this takes shape as an event".

   ....

   ....

   ....

2. In your own words explain what you think Reeves means by "The reader's experience has been permanently enlarged." (lines 42–3).

   ....

   ....

3. In your own words explain what you think Clarke means when she says the subject of a poem is an "excuse to rummage in the mind for language". (lines 13–14)

   ....

   ....

4. Clarke says a poem has to be "unmade and made again in the cold light of the mind before it can be called a finished work of art" (lines 22–4). Do you think all creative writing requires this process, or just poetry? Explain your thoughts.

   ....

   ....

   ....

5. Why, in your opinion, does Clarke say "To have an idea for a poem is to have nothing at all."? (lines 24–5)

   ....

   ....

6. The two poets talk about where poems come from in different ways. Is there any point on which they agree? Explain your thoughts.

   ....

   ....

   ....

   ....

   ....

   ....

Developing language appreciation: a poet's choice of words

White Sails of a Regatta

Early morning, warm at the north end
Of the Mar Menor, near a graveyard
Of small boats, colour of flaky bone.

Close to the broken hulls a few
Working boats are moored to life.   5
An old fish net yawns in the heat

On its drying-rack of spindly poles,
Its cross-struts parallel to the sea's surface
Are like grave markers against the sun.

I feel this is a movie scene not moving.   10
A seascape in still-life close-up.
On another old rack three nets drape

Like mourning shawls from its shoulder,
Weather, salt and water tatter it.
Light flickers fractals through the mesh.   15

Above flaked broken bodies of boats
Terns mock the air in stabbing flights
Mugging fish from one beak after another.

I sit on the beach taking it all in.
To my left an old man in orange waders   20
Untangles his worn net, mesh by mesh.

In a break for his fingers he tells me it has rotted
For years. He wonders if it's worth the trouble.
But adds that it gets him out of the house,

Out of his wife's hair as she prepares   25
   Sunday lunch.
We watch a sleek modern canoe pass silently
As the light wind drops to nothing.

Some metres offshore the Mar Menor glares.
Fills our eyes with painful light. The boats are
our still life. Like backlit graveyard furniture.   30

Under the surface some other world is pulling
Sunlight down to its own spectrum of shallows,
Fishermen, histories of catches. A few swallows

Sweep by, low over water, moving as fast
As their upside-down images allow. They go   35
Out beyond each boat dead or alive

To where the water is now blueing darkly
Below sails of a Regatta out of La Ribera.
Bright, triangular, against the Scoured Landscape.

Over there, southwest of here   40
Murcia airport's new control tower
Is merely a fuzzy thistlehead

While right in this foreground here
Reflections of an emerald green hull
Move silently like a pool of thick sap.   45

Green dips, then under sea-blue it seems.
A gust of wind scatters a bracelet of light loose,
Like bent ovals of water I've seen on lochs.

Here, each flaking boat, and each living hull
Rocks like sad seaweed in a slow, slow tide.   50
One peeling boat shrouded in its ruin of white

'La Virgen de Caridad', no longer sways.
She is laid here, falling apart, no rest in peace.
No bracelets of oval light now touch her.

Terns dive between her broken ribs.   55
The Regatta sails look like hooded mourners
Moving slowly in the heat-haze of Murcia.

By Neil MacNeil (1940–)

Regatta: boat or yacht races.

Mar Menor: a stretch of the Spanish Mediterranean coastline.

Lochs: Scottish lakes.

Murcia: the Spanish province of Murcia, where the Mar Menor is located.

Waders: thigh-high waterproof boots.

1. Explain how and why the poet uses the following words and phrases. You may quote from the poem to support your answers.

   a. "a graveyard / Of small boats" (lines 2/3)

   ....

   ....

   ....

   b. "a movie scene not moving" (line 10)

   ....

   ....

   ....

   c. "painful light" (line 29)

   ....

   ....

   ....

   d. "A gust of wind scatters a bracelet of light loose, / Like bent ovals of water" (lines 47/48).

   ....

   ....

   ....

2. Write a paragraph about how the words and images in "White Sails of a Regatta" convey a sense of time passing and/or sadness.

   ....

   ....

   ....

   ....

   ....

   ....

Reminder

Although there are no poems in the exams, reading poetry helps you to understand how words work and how words and phrases can be used to convey a tone or atmosphere.

8 World famous

Preparing for Reading Passages (Core)

Read the following information posted on the Internet about the importance of taking safety seriously while climbing the mountain Mont Blanc in France. Then answer the question that follows.

Is Mont Blanc the World's most dangerous mountain?

28 January 2009

I remember standing on the small hill behind the Tete Rousse hut looking at the Gouter face of Mont Blanc, our proposed line of ascent. We were guiding a party of four clients and had guided on this [part of the mountain] many times in the 5 past. This particular time was only two days after heavy snowfall and the face was seething with activity. Avalanches seemingly were coming down at random every 5 or 10 minutes. As we watched two climbers crossed the Grand Couloir. Halfway 10 across, they started running as an avalanche came down the chute. They narrowly made it, escaping with their lives. A close call.

I informed my clients that, as they could see, the face was too dangerous to attempt in the 15 current conditions. We should turn back and do something else. "Why?" came the reply. "They have just gone up," he said pointing to the two lucky climbers. Another remarked, "My mate did it last year and said it was just a snow plod". 20 They were not happy that I was not prepared to play Russian Roulette with their lives!

I came across this interesting article by Stewart Green in the "Guide to Climbing" at About.com. 25

Mont Blanc is dangerous. No doubt about that. Four Italians killed last week on the Aiguille du Midi. And the two young Britons were killed the previous weekend in the Gervasutti. It's difficult to find overall statistics on climbing accidents in the Alps because stats are kept by each country and what is included varies widely. But local guides and rescue groups say there are many reasons why so many climbers die on Mont Blanc. Many die because of subjective reasons such as unpreparedness, not bringing the right equipment and clothing, lack of experience and bad judgment. The others die for objective reasons including avalanches, falling rocks, blizzards and bad weather. [...]

Mont Blanc, a huge mountain massif straddling the French and Italian border, is simply the most dangerous mountain in the world. Lots of people are killed and injured on it every year, and still they come in hordes to ascend to the roof of Europe. Why? Because the climbing is that good.

Some of the reasons are basically the same as those outlined in a 1902 article in the *New York Times*. The article cited a study of accidents from 1890 to 1901 by the Swiss Alpine Club, which found that 303 alpinists were killed in the Alps in that period. The study noted that the immediate causes of death included not employing a guide; climbing unknown routes from late fall to spring; foolhardy adventurousness, vanity, the spirit of emulation, want of experience and even absentmindedness!

Okay, maybe the last reason is not as valid these days, but still lots of people die on Mont Blanc. Over 20,000 people reach its summit each year, mostly via the easier normal routes, which are still deadly. On peak weekends in late July and August, the local rescue services fly at least a dozen missions rescuing climbers or picking up the dead. Still they come, climbing and dying.

[...] Having climbed the mountain many times we find that the 1,800ft Gouter Ridge on the approach to the Gouter hut, as loose and exposed to rock avalanches as it is, is still ascended in the main by helmetless climbers; these same climbers crossing and eventually recrossing the dangerous Grand Couloir whilst disdaining the use of basic, safety equipment.

30
35
40
45
50
55
60
65
70

Reminder

Approach the question in the following way:

- Find relevant information and annotate the text.
- Think about what you have read and add your own thoughts.
- Read between the lines and develop both the information provided and what you have inferred from the writer's words.

Imagine you are planning a summer holiday on Mont Blanc with a climbing group. You read this online article about Mont Blanc and decide to write an information leaflet for the members of your group.

In your information sheet you should:

- explain the potential dangers of climbing at high altitude during summer months

- comment on why safety precautions should be taken seriously

- express your thoughts on why being cautious will not spoil the excitement of climbing on the highest mountain in Europe.

Base your information on what you have read in the passage. Use your own words as a far as possible. You do not need to write in columns or create a layout for the leaflet.

Write between 200 and 300 words. Use a separate sheet of paper if necessary.

Preparing for Reading Passages (Extended)

Read the passage and then answer the question that follows.

The passage is a report from the online Ski Channel about a summer avalanche in the French Alps. You will need to think about the dangers and the importance of taking safety seriously.

Mont Blanc Avalanche

By Shannon Marie Quirk, Ski Channel

An avalanche in the French Alps on Thursday, July 12, 2012 swept a large crew of European climbers down the Mount Maudit slope leading to Mont Blanc, accounting for nine deaths, at least eleven hospitalized and several others unaccounted for, authorities said. Rescue teams are still searching for the missing. 5

First reports of the wipeout on Mont Maudit came at 5:25 a.m. when the climbers were about a thousand feet from the summit of the 14,649 foot mountain, NY Daily News.com reported. 10

"We were initially alerted just after dawn by one of the survivors who called us on a mobile phone," said Bertrand François of the local gendarmerie.

Dozens of gendarmes were furiously searching through the snow for survivors of the doomed expedition that included 28 climbers from Britain, Denmark, France, Germany, Serbia, Spain and Switzerland, officials said. 15

The mayor of Chamonix, Eric Fournier, is referring to the catastrophe as "one of the deadliest avalanches in recent years [...] There was no weather bulletin giving any avalanche warning," he told *The Guardian*. 20

A climber trying to scale Mont Blanc accidently caused a slab of ice to snap off on Thursday high in the French Alps, sparking an avalanche. As a sheet of snow and ice thundered down the steep slope, several other climbers managed to turn away from the slide in time, regional authorities in Haute-Savoie said. 25 30

Two other climbers were rescued as emergency crews using dogs and helicopters scoured the churned-up, high-altitude area in a frantic search for the missing. Their quest, hampered by the possibility of further avalanches, was called off before nightfall. 35

Three Britons, three Germans and two Spaniards were among the dead, their governments confirmed. The other victim was from Switzerland, according to the gendarme service in the French mountain town of Chamonix. 40

Early summer storms apparently left behind heavy snow that combined with high winds to form dangerous overhanging conditions on some of the popular climbing routes around Mont Blanc, the highest mountain in Western Europe. Regional authorities had warned climbers earlier this summer to be careful because of an unusually snowy spring. 45 50

The Mont Blanc massif is a popular area for climbers, hikers and tourists but a dangerous one, with dozens dying on it each year. Chamonix, a top center for climbing, hosted the first Winter Olympics in 1924. 55

Some of the climbers were with professional guides, others were climbing independently.

The gendarme service said it was alerted around 5:25 a.m. Thursday to the avalanche, which hit a group of climbers—ones from Switzerland, Germany, Spain, France, Denmark and Serbia—some 4,000 meters (13,100 feet) high on the north face of Mont Maudit, part of the Mont Blanc range. 60

A block of ice some 40 centimeters (16 inches) thick broke off and slid down the slope, creating a mass of snow that was 2 meters (6-foot) deep and 50 meters (160 feet) long. 65

"The first elements that we have from testimony are that a climber could have set loose a sheet of ice, and that sheet then pulled down the group of climbers below. I should say that the incline is very, very steep on this northern face," Col. Bertrand François of the Haute-Savoie gendarme service told reporters. 70 75

It was not immediately known if the climber lived or died.

According to recent tweets from climbers, high winds led to overhanging ice slabs forming on the slope. Several days ago Chamonix saw a 80 monsoon-like downpour which turned to snow at 3,000 meters (9,850 feet) high.

Jonas Moestrup from the western Danish city of Randers heard about the accident as he was on his way down from Mont Blanc. 85

"Three days ago, we ascended it (Mont Maudit). It was shocking to hear, it could easily have been us," he told the Danish news agency Ritzau by telephone. "It is scary and tragic."

Still, he noted the allure of those foreboding, 90 majestic Alpine peaks. "It's part of the thrill that something can go wrong," he told Ritzau.

French Interior Minister Manuel Valls flew over the site later on Thursday, describing it as "a particularly spectacular block of ice". He said the 95 climbers appeared to be an experienced group and that the churned-up snow had made the search particularly difficult.

You are a climber who has survived the Mont Blanc avalanche. Write an interview with a journalist where you explain what you think happened and how you escaped injury. Write between 250 and 350 words.

In your interview you should comment on:

- the dangers of hiking at high altitude on Mont Blanc
- what you think happened to cause the avalanche
- the weather conditions
- how you felt.
- why climbers and hikers should take safety precautions seriously.

Begin your interview:

Journalist: I understand you just made it to safety. Can you tell me what happened?

Me: …

Use the lines on the next page and a separate sheet of paper if necessary.

Reminder

This type of question asks you to demonstrate your understanding of the text and implicit meanings (what is inferred), and to evaluate what you have read, giving your ideas and opinions.

Using English: persuasive language

Here are two famous speeches made during the 19th century in the USA. Read them carefully and then look at how the speakers try to persuade their audiences to their way of thinking.

This first speech was made impromptu (without preparation or notes) by an ex-slave named Sojourner Truth at the Women's Convention in Akron, Ohio in 1851. When it was published in 1863 by Frances Gage it was given the title 'Ain't I a Woman?'

Sojourner Truth (1797–1883) was born in slavery but escaped with her infant daughter in 1826. Apart from giving this moving speech, she became famous for being the first black woman to ever win a court case against a white man.

Ain't I a woman?

Well, children, where there is so much racket there must be something out of kilter. I think that 'twixt the negroes of the South and the women at the North, all talking about rights, the white men will be in a fix pretty soon. But what's all this here 5 talking about?

That man over there says that women need to be helped into carriages, and lifted over ditches, and to have the best place everywhere. Nobody ever helps me into carriages, or over mud- 10 puddles, or gives me any best place! And ain't I a woman? Look at me! Look at my arm! I have ploughed and planted, and gathered into barns, and no man could head me! And ain't I a woman? I could work as much and eat as much as a 15 man – when I could get it – and bear the lash as well! And ain't I a woman? I have borne thirteen children, and seen most all sold off to slavery, and when I cried out with my mother's grief, none but Jesus heard me! And ain't I a woman? 20

Then they talk about this thing in the head; what's this they call it? [member of audience whispers, "intellect"] That's it, honey. What's that got to do with women's rights or negroes' rights? If my cup won't hold but a pint, and yours holds a 25 quart, wouldn't you be mean not to let me have my little half measure full?

Then that little man in black there, he says women can't have as much rights as men, 'cause Christ wasn't a woman! Where did your Christ 30 come from? Where did your Christ come from? From God and a woman! Man had nothing to do with Him.

If the first woman God ever made was strong enough to turn the world upside down all alone, 35 these women together ought to be able to turn it back, and get it right side up again! And now they is asking to do it, the men better let them.

Obliged to you for hearing me, and now old Sojourner ain't got nothing more to say. 40

The famous American president Abraham Lincoln gave this speech on the 9 November 1863 at the dedication of the Soldiers' National Cemetery at Gettysburg, the site of one of the bloodiest battles in the American Civil War. In this short speech Lincoln calls upon the principles of human equality and dignity contained in the Declaration of Independence and connects the sacrifices made on both sides fighting in Civil War. He expresses the American desire for "a new birth of freedom" and the importance of preserving the self-governing Union that was created in 1776.

Lincoln was the second person to address the crowd that day: the first speaker was a famed orator named Edward Everett, who spoke for two hours. The following day Everett wrote to Lincoln saying, "Permit me also to express my great admiration of the thoughts expressed by you, with such eloquent simplicity and appropriateness, at the consecration of the Cemetery. I should be glad, if I could flatter myself that I came as near to the central idea of the occasion, in two hours, as you did in two minutes."

Gettysburg Address

Fourscore and seven years ago our fathers brought forth on this continent a new nation, conceived in liberty and dedicated to the proposition that all men are created equal.

Now we are engaged in a great civil war, 5
testing whether that nation or any nation so conceived and so dedicated can long endure. We are met on a great battlefield of that war. We have come to dedicate a portion of that field as a final resting-place for those who here gave their lives 10
that that nation might live. It is altogether fitting and proper that we should do this.

But, in a larger sense, we cannot dedicate, we cannot consecrate, we cannot hallow this ground. The brave men, living and dead who struggled 15
here have consecrated it far above our poor power to add or detract. The world will little note nor long remember what we say here, but it can never forget what they did here. It is for us the living rather to be dedicated here to the unfinished 20
work which they who fought here have thus far so nobly advanced. It is rather for us to be here dedicated to the great task remaining before us – that from these honored dead we take increased devotion to that cause for which they gave the last full 25
measure of devotion – that we here highly resolve that these dead shall not have died in vain, that this nation under God shall have a new birth of freedom, and that government of the people, by the people, for the people shall not perish from the earth. 30

Reminder

Rhetorical questions show the audience the situation so that the answer offered seems to be the only right thing to do.

Rule of three (tripling) gives three examples to reinforce a point, using powerful adjectives, so the audience remembers it.

Alliteration helps to make words memorable, e.g. **We will win this war!**

Hyperbole exaggerates the bad, accentuates the good so the audience can 'feel' that experience.

Including the audience (using e.g. *us*, *we*, *together*) addresses them directly, uniting them and making them feel they belong together with the speaker.

Destroying the opposition's argument in a polite and reasonable way works best.

Emotive language affects the way the audience feels, e.g. making them sad or sorry, offering them hope and making them want to take action.

Using the techniques in the Reminder box, answer the following questions. Quote from the speeches to support your views.

1. How does Sojourner Truth include her audience?

    ....

    ....

2. Why is this so significant in her speech?

    ....

    ....

3. How does Abraham Lincoln use the tripling technique?

    ....

    ....

4. How does Lincoln include his audience?

    ....

    ....

5. Why, in your opinion, is this important in Lincoln's speech?

    ....

    ....

6. Explain how and why Sojourner Truth uses the rhetorical question "Ain't I a woman?".

    ....

    ....

    ....

    ....

    ....

    ....

    ....

    ....

    ....

    ....

    ....

    ....

    ....

    ....

    ....

    ....

    ....

    ....

    ....

7. Sojourner Truth's impromtu speech was so important that it was written down and published. Select words and phrases from her speech and explain how they may have affected listeners at the time. Quote from the speech and explain the effects of her words.

....

....

....

....

8. The Gettysburg Address is still famous today. Select words and phrases from Lincoln's speech to explain how they may have affected listeners at the time. Quote from the speech and explain the effects of his words.

....

....

....

....

9. Using either Sojourner Truth's speech or Lincoln's address as a model, write a paragraph for a speech on something about which you feel strongly.

Aim to persuade your audience to your way of thinking as briefly and effectively as possible.

....

....

....

....

....

....

....

....

....

....

....

....

....

....

....

....

....

9 Endings

Practising reading skills

Read each of the following fiction passages and time how long it takes you to read it. After reading each passage, answer the reading comprehension questions that follow. Time how long it takes you to make notes and answer each question.

In this first passage you hear the voice of 11-year-old Laurie talking about his teacher, Miss Glennie. The school is in a fictional town in the north-east of England. As you read, underline words or phrases and make notes in the margin on how the author presents the scene from a child's point of view.

The narrator's voice

At last there has been something really good happening at my new school. We had a sort of a history lesson and Miss Glennie told us about boy chimney sweeps. She has got a book like the books in my father's study (only his are thicker 5 and the writing is much, much smaller) and I think books like that are about a hundred years old. She reads a bit out of this book and then we talk about it. She was reading today about the way of training a climbing boy, which is what 10 they used to call the sweeps' boys; how to wash their knees in salty water and scrub their knees with a hard brush every day, so no matter how much they scrape inside the chimney it will not hurt. It does at first, of course. In those days their 15 trousers went into rags quite quickly, so they cut themselves on the stones of the chimneys.

When it was the time for the whole class to discuss this, I was the first one to ask things. Did they bleed a lot? How did the sweep find the boys 20 when they had finished? Did the boys die? Were they my size? Why did they climb if it hurt?

Miss Glennie said other people should have a chance to ask questions. Micka said he would have run away. 25

"But Michael," Miss Glennie said in her kind and soft voice, "these poor boys had no choice. For them, it was work or starve. Sometimes it was their own fathers who were the sweeps and they beat them to make them climb higher." 30

I asked again – Why did they climb if it hurt and their knees were bleeding like you said? Why didn't they come down again?

Miss Glennie opened her eyes wide.

"The sweeps would light a fire in the grate of 35 the chimney when the boys were up, to make them go faster. They would breathe the smoke and get scared of choking. So the boys would climb quickly to the top so they could breathe the fresh air. Sometimes the smoke made them too dizzy 40 to hold on any longer, and they let go and fell into the fire."

"Why didn't their mothers come and save them?" Lisa Carmichael asked that. What a stupid question to ask; such a girl question. All the other 45 girls looked as if they were going to be sick. Miss Glennie's voice got very sad and she said, "Very often they were orphans. They didn't have mothers."

Now, that is what I call a good lesson. If every day was like that I would be at school more often. 50 Unfortunately, then Miss Glennie made us do some writing about "I am a climbing boy (or girl, even though girls did not do it but at school we must always say girls can do anything boys can do, even if it is something cruel that hurts, like climbing 55 chimneys) and what are my feelings about chimney sweeping." This could have ruined a brilliant lesson, except I didn't do the writing, just a kind of a cartoon picture of a sweep lighting a huge fire with a most evil grin on his wicked face, 60 and in the next picture a little skinny boy climbing up and up, with a balloon coming out of his mouth saying, "Can't breathe, choking, cough cough." The boy looked like Micka. I showed it to him but he said my drawing was rubbish. Miss Glennie gave 65 me a green star for the picture (of course), but she put underneath; "Where is your writing, Laurie?". She is too soft. A real teacher would have torn up the picture and kept me in as a punishment.

From *Micka*, by Frances Kay

Sweeps' boys: until the late 19th century, the boys who climbed chimneys to clear the soot out for the men (sweeps) employed to clean chimneys.

Consecrate: to declare as sacred or holy.

Hallow: to consecrate or make holy.

1. Using two examples from the passage to support your ideas, explain how the author presents this scene from Laurie's point of view.

   ....
   ....
   ....

2. The narrator, Laurie, asks the teacher why a boy continued to climb a chimney if it made his knees bleed. In your own words explain the teacher's response to this question.

   ....
   ....
   ....

3. One girl asks a question. What is the narrator's reaction to her question?

   ....

   ....

   ....

4. Why, in your opinion, does Laurie not do the writing task as the teacher requested?

   ....

   ....

5. Miss Glennie gives Laurie a green star for his cartoon picture although it is not what she asked the class to do. In your opinion why does she do this?

   ....

   ....

6. You are Miss Glennie. Your head teacher wants a short report on Laurie. Summarise Laurie's behaviour, attitude and class work in your lessons. Write about 200 words.

   ....

   ....

   ....

   ....

   ....

   ....

   ....

   ....

   ....

   ....

   ....

   ....

   ....

   ....

   ....

   ....

   ....

   ....

   ....

   ....

Now read two passages about a young girl living in France during the
Second World War. In Passage A nine-year-old Boise wants to go to the
cinema with her older brother Cassis and sister Reinette (Reine). She can
only go if she can pay for her ticket. Boise hasn't got any money, but she
knows where to find some. She prepares to raid Cassis' "Treasure Chest".

Passage A: Treasure Chest

At five in the morning the Loire is still and
sumptuous with mist. The water is beautiful at
that time of the day, cool and magically pale, the
sandbanks rising like lost continents. The water
smells of night, and here and there a spray of new   5
sunlight makes mica shadows on the surface.
I took off my shoes and my dress and surveyed
the water critically. It looked deceptively still.

The last of the Standing Stones, the Treasure
Stone, was maybe thirty feet from the bank, and   10
the water at its base looked oddly silky at the
surface, a sign that a strong current was at work.
I could drown here, I told myself suddenly, and no
one would even know where to look for me.

But I had no choice. Cassis had issued a   15
challenge. I had to pay my own way. How could I
do that, with no pocket money of my own, without
using the purse hidden in the Treasure Chest? Of
course, there was a chance he might have removed
it. If he had, I would risk stealing from my   20
mother's purse. But that I was reluctant to do. Not
because stealing was especially wrong, but because
of my mother's unusual memory for figures. She
knew what she had to the last centime, and she
would know at once what I had done.   25

No. It had to be the Treasure Chest.

Since Cassis and Reinette had finished school
there had been few expeditions to the river. They
had treasure of their own – *adult* treasure – to
gloat over. The few coins in the purse amounted   30

to a couple of francs, no more. I was counting on
Cassis' laziness, his conviction that no one but he
would be able to reach the box tied to the pillar.
I was sure the money was still there.

Carefully, I scrambled down the bank and   35
into the water. It was cold and river mud oozed
between my toes. I waded out until the water was
waist deep. I could feel the current now, like an
impatient dog at the leash. God, it was already
so strong! I put out a hand against the first pillar,   40
pushing away from it into the current, and took
another step. I knew there was a drop just ahead,
a point at which the still-shallow verge of the
Loire sheared away into nothingness. Cassis,
when he was making the trip, always pretended   45
to drown at this point, turning belly-up into the
opaque water, struggling and screaming, with a
mouthful of brown Loire spurting from between
his lips. He always fooled Reine, however many
times he did this, making her squeal in horror as   50
he sank beneath the surface.

I had no time for such an exhibition. I felt for
the drop with my toes. There. Pushing against
the riverbed, I propelled myself as far as I could
with my first kick, keeping the Standing Stones   55
downriver to my right.

From *Five Quarters of the Orange*,
by Joanne Harris

1. Where is the Treasure Chest?

   ....

   ....

2. What does the Treasure Chest contain?

   ....

   ....

3. Why does Boise not want to risk taking money from her mother's purse?

   ....

   ....

4. Find two examples in Passage A to show what Boise is doing is dangerous.

   ....

   ....

   ....

5. Why, in your opinion, does the author include the information that Cassis "always pretended to drown at this point, turning belly-up" in lines 45–6?

   ....

   ....

6. Why, from Boise's point of view, is it necessary to swim out to the Treasure Chest?

   ....

   ....

7. In your own words explain how and why the reader fears for Boise's safety.

   ....

   ....

   ....

   ....

Passage B: Treasure Chest

The water was warmer on the surface, and the drag of current not as strong. I swam steadily, in a smooth arc, from the first Standing Stone to the second. The stones were maybe twelve feet apart at their widest stretch, spread unevenly 5 from the bank. I could make five feet with a good strong kick against each pillar, aiming slightly upstream so the current would bring me back to the next pillar in time to begin again. Like a small boat tacking against a strong wind, I limped 10 towards the Treasure Stone, feeling the current grow stronger each time. I was gasping with cold. Then I was at the fourth pillar, making my final lunge towards my goal. As the current dragged me towards the Treasure Stone I overshot the 15 pillar, and there was a moment of sudden, sparkling terror as I began to move downstream into the main drag of the river, my arms and legs pinwheeling against the water. Panting, almost crying with panic, I managed to kick myself 20 within range of the stone, and grabbed the chain that secured the Treasure Chest to the pillar. It felt weedy and unpleasant in my hand, slimed with the brown ooze of the river, but I used it to manoeuvre myself around the pillar. 25

I clung there for a moment, letting my pounding heart quiet. Then, with my back wedged safely against the pillar, I hauled the Treasure Chest up and out of its muddy cradle. It was a difficult job. The box itself was not especially 30 heavy, but weighted with chain and tarpaulin as it was, it seemed a dead weight. Trembling with cold now, my teeth clattering, I struggled with the chain and finally felt something give. Kicking my

legs frantically to keep my position against the 35 pillar, I hauled at the box. I knew another moment of near panic as the mud-slimed tarpaulin caught at my feet, then my fingers were working at the rope which held the box. For an instant I was sure my numbed fingers would not be able to open the 40 tin, then the catch gave way and water rushed into the Treasure Chest. I swore. Still, there was the purse, an old brown leather thing Mother had discarded because of a faulty catch. I grabbed it and jammed it between my teeth for safety, then, 45 with a final effort, I slammed the box closed and let it sink, weighted by its chain, to the bottom again. The tarpaulin was lost, of course, the remaining treasure waterlogged, but that couldn't be helped. Cassis would have to find somewhere 50 drier to hide his cigarettes. I had the money, and that was all that mattered.

I swam back to the bank, missing the last two pillars and drifting 200 yards down towards the Angers road before I managed to steer myself out 55 of the current, which was now more like a dog than ever, a mad, brown dog with its leash twined crazily around my frozen legs. The whole episode, I guessed, had taken maybe ten minutes.

I forced myself to rest awhile, feeling the slight 60 warmth of the sun's first rays on my face, drying the mud of the Loire on my skin. I was trembling with cold and exhilaration. I counted the money in the purse; there was certainly enough for a cinema ticket and a glass of squash. 65

From *Five Quarters of the Orange*,
by Joanne Harris

Tarpaulin: a waterproof sheet material used to protect things from moisture.

1. Find ten points in Passage B that explain how Boise finally obtains the money she needs to go to the cinema and the difficulties she encounters in getting back to safety.

   Write your answer in short notes here. (You do not have to write in sentences.) Use a separate sheet of paper if necessary.

....
....
....
....
....
....
....
....
....
....
....
....
....
....
....
....
....
....
....
....
....
....
....
....
....
....
....
....
....

2. Use your notes to summarise what Passage B tells you about how Boise obtains money to go to the cinema and the difficulties she encounters in getting back to safety.

Include the ten points in your notes. Use continuous writing (not note form) and use your own words as far as possible. Write about 200 words. Use a separate sheet of paper if necessary.

....

....

....

....

....

....

....

....

....

....

....

....

....

....

....

....

....

....

....

....

....

....

....

....

....

....

....

10 Exam practice

Preparing for Reading Passages (Core)

Read the article below carefully and then answer the summary questions that follow.

Lang Lang: The Pied Piper pianist of China

By Susie Mesure, *The Independent Online*
(22 May 2011)

Be kind, global star urges parents, as budding musicians vie to join him.

He was a piano prodigy who flourished despite the extreme pressure doled out by his ambitious father, but today Lang Lang warns pushy   5
parents to back off if they want to nurture their offspring's talent.

His rebuke will come as a salutary lesson in childcare for hundreds of parents tempted to step up the hot housing after watching 100 budding   10
musicians – aged as young as six – take the main stage with the superstar maestro at London's Southbank Centre this afternoon.

Lang, a global sensation at 28 years old, learnt the hard way about the perils of parental   15
coercion: aged just nine, he was urged to kill himself by his tyrannical father for missing two hours of practice. Yesterday he told *The Independent on Sunday* that parents needed to strike a careful "balance between being strict   20
and loosening up".

He added: "I want to tell parents who put their kids under a lot of pressure, 'This is not the way to do it'. I want people to learn this is not the way to be successful. To give your whole passion – yes;   25
to give up a life – no. There's a balance."

[...] He would certainly raise any eventual children of his own somewhat differently. "For sure," he laughed nervously: "I'd be very different from my father. I'd let the kids decide what they wanted to do."   30

The youngsters making up Lang's 51-strong Piano Orchestra today include six-year-old Alastair Howell [who is] one of 12 hand-picked by the Chinese star out of more than 500 hopefuls who applied to be part of the ensemble. Lang said he   35
hoped to be able to mentor the most promising

pianists – either with a repeat collaboration next year or something more permanent.

[...] Then there are the 50-odd Brazilians who make up the Youth Orchestra of Bahia, which 40 played with Lang last night. Plucked off the street in one of the poorest parts of Brazil, these impressive teenagers have only been playing their instruments for the past three or so years. I catch them practising [...] they are conducted by the 45 17-year-old Venezuelan Ilyich Rivas. It's only a rehearsal but the atmosphere is electric as they zip through the Chopin and Gershwin concertos they play with the virtuoso.

[...] Lang [...] regards himself as something of 50 a missionary when it comes to inspiring others,

regardless of their nationality. "Music is for the world," he tells me earnestly, in his heavily accented English. "As musicians, we are citizens of the world and we need to really share our love 55 and passion with everyone."

While he is keen to stress that success must not come at too heavy a price, he does admit that there are no shortcuts to reaching the top. "Everybody can achieve their dream in different 60 ways, but unfortunately in the music world there is one way to be successful, which is to never stop practising. This is something you can't avoid, no matter how talented you are. I made my career today through really hard practice." 65

1. What is the Chinese pianist Lang Lang doing to promote young musicians and what are his thoughts and feelings about parents who push their children to practise too much?

   Write your answers in short notes on the lines provided. You do not need to use your own words. Up to 10 marks are available for the content of your answer.

   - ....
   - ....
   - ....
   - ....
   - ....
   - ....
   - ....
   - ....
   - ....
   - ....
   - ....
   - ....
   - ....
   - ....
   - ....

2. Use your notes to summarise what the passage tells you about what the Chinese pianist Lang Lang is doing to promote young musicians, and about his thoughts and feelings about parents who push their children to practise too much.

Use continuous writing (not note form) and use your own words as far as possible. Your summary should include all ten points from your notes and must be between 100 and 150 words. Use a separate sheet of paper if necessary.

....

....

....

....

....

....

....

....

....

....

....

....

....

....

....

....

....

....

....

....

....

....

....

....

....

....

....

....

Preparing for Reading Passages (Extended)

Read the article below carefully and then answer the question that follows.

We can't all be Mozart – but we can still play

From "Caracas to Stirling, the evidence that music can transform lives is utterly overwhelming", by Jesse Norman, *The Telegraph* (24 June 2012)

Today the renowned Simón Bolívar Symphony Orchestra and its dazzling conductor Gustavo Dudamel are coming to town. But the town isn't London […] it's Raploch, a tough estate on the outskirts of Stirling in Scotland, where the 5 "Bolívars" will be playing a concert in front of 8,000 people.

Raploch has long been notorious for poverty and crime. Four years ago only one child among the 3,000 people living there learned a musical 10 instrument. Now it's 450. That's because the estate has become the testing ground for Sistema Scotland: an extraordinary social experiment aiming to transform a community by immersing it in music. And it seems to be working. 15

The experiment originated as El Sistema in Venezuela 37 years ago, teaching children to play orchestral music in groups, and so to build self-discipline and teamwork. These days more than 300,000 young people are enrolled; 80–90 percent 20 of them from poorer backgrounds, in particular the shanty towns around Caracas. As violence and gang warfare engulf the country – with 53 murders a day in the capital last year – El Sistema has become a crucial source of peace and 25 stability for many families.

How can this be? Music is a deep mystery. But […] music confers a huge range of cognitive, behavioural, emotional, therapeutic and social benefits. It offers models of discipline and 30 focused practice whose value is now being understood by scientists and management theorists alike. It encourages aspiration to reach the highest standards. It is open to all, and no respecter of persons. It can be hugely competitive, or intensely 35 co-operative. Occasionally individualistic, it is more often about teamwork and shared spirit. Its value flows past individuals into families and society. But to enjoy the benefits fully, you have to do it. You can't be a couch potato. 40

Other countries understand the social power of music far better than we do. El Sistema is one example. Finland has long had a comprehensive musical culture, which has resulted in a profusion of world-class talent from a country of just over 45 five million people. It may be no coincidence that Finnish schoolchildren are, on almost every measure, some of the best educated in the world.

Unfortunately, for all its pervasiveness and passion, music is set about with myth and 50 misunderstanding. An Amadeus [Mozart] mythology has grown up in which musical talent is thought to be a divine gift to a few favoured souls, from which the rest of us are and must ever be excluded. […] 55

The truth is that virtually everyone has innate musical ability, but that ability fades if it is not used and developed. Of course, lessons and instruments cost money. But properly understood, the lesson of El Sistema is that music is not an 60 elitist activity open only to the wealthy few, but a massively empowering activity for the many. The classical music tradition is one of the greatest glories of human culture; but so is that of jazz or of Indian raga. 65

Thirty years ago there was little public understanding of the social value of sport; now it is a commonplace. Why not with music? Yet there is an important difference between sport and music. Sport is fundamentally about aggression, 70 competition and winning. […] music is about teamwork, joy, mutual respect and ultimately love. The Raploch experiment hasn't finished yet. It's not cheap, but its annual cost is less than 1 per cent of the price of keeping a young person in 75 secure accommodation.

Imagine you are a music teacher in an inner-city school with serious behaviour problems and high absenteeism. You read the article about El Sistema in Venezuela and Sistema Scotland in Raploch, and decide you would like to start something similar in your school.

Write a letter to your Head or Principal describing El Sistema and how it might help your school. Include the following points:

- how and why El Sistema started in Venezuela
- how Sistema Scotland has benefited Raploch
- your views on how music can help young people
- your thoughts on starting an orchestra at your school.

Base your ideas on information found in the passage. Write between 250 and 350 words. Use a separate sheet of paper if necessary.

....

....

....

....

....

....

....

....

....

....

....

....

....

....

....

....

....

....

....

....

....

....

Preparing for Directed Writing and Composition (Core and Extended)

Read the following passages about English pantomimes and then answer the Directed Writing and Composition questions that follow.

What a pantomime!

British pantomime is a traditional winter entertainment, a musical comedy with topical humour, popular celebrities and television stars. Modern pantomimes are still based on traditional fairy stories such as *Cinderella*, *Aladdin*, *Dick Whittington*, *Snow White*. Scriptwriters add contemporary references to politics, sport and television, and provide plenty of opportunity for audiences to get involved in the action. Pantomimes are colourful, noisy, good fun and great family entertainment. In fact they're a must for any family.

    British pantomime dates back to 15th- and 16th-century traditions of *Comedia dell'arte* in which there are stock characters and stage conventions. In every pantomime there is:

- a principal boy played by a girl with long legs in a tight costume
- the pantomime dame, who's a man in women's clothes that no woman would ever wear
- a chorus figure, the principal boy's brother or friend, who speaks directly to the audience
- an animal usually a cow played by two actors in one costume
- a villain, who is hissed at by the audience
- lots of audience participation that includes shouting, "Look behind you!" and the traditional "Oh yes it is!" – "Oh no it isn't!" routine.

5

10

15

20

Cinderella at The Townhouse Theatre!

Book early for this year's spectacular pantomime and bring all the family …

If you're in England this winter, "Look Behind you!"

The lights go down, the audience falls silent. Suddenly, there's billowing smoke and a "baddie" rather like a nasty red devil emerges from the left, the sinister side of the stage. The baddie sneers and curses the characters we're about to meet, listing 5
the awful things he'd like to happen to them.

"Not so fast," says a beautiful fairy, drifting onto the stage (in a harness) from above and waving her sparkly wand. Little girls gasp at her costume and the adults are comforted – good will 10
once more triumph over evil.

And another pantomime has begun! Another generation of children is being drawn into the fantastic, hilarious and sometimes very naughty world of this very English holiday entertainment. 15

Pantomime is full of stock characters, none of whom can be omitted because pantomime-goers expect to see a romantic couple in the form of a beautiful maiden or princess and a "principal boy", who's actually a girl in tights, playing the 20
hero. And there has to be a pantomime dame! The dame, probably the best-loved character of all, is always played by a man in show-stopping, outrageous dresses!

Pantomimes are based on traditional fairy 25
tales. Take *Aladdin*, which features the lamp-discovering boy (played by a woman, of course), a lovely princess, the wicked uncle and Aladdin's mother, Widow Twanky (the dame), who runs a laundry and has been a favourite for centuries. 30
Other popular stories are *Cinderella*, *Jack and the Beanstalk* and *Snow White*, *Sleeping Beauty* and *Babes in the Wood*.

One of the earliest pantomimes was *Robinson Crusoe*. This show, which first played in 1778 at 35
the Theatre Royal, Drury Lane in London, wove in stock characters from Italian *Commedia dell'arte*: Harlequin, Columbine and the clown Pantaloon (introduced to British audiences more than 100 years earlier), with the shipwrecked mariner 40
Crusoe and his companion, Man Friday. This mixture of characters with a British-based plotline established the foundation for stock characters.

The 1778 production, incidentally, included a young actor called Joseph Grimaldi, who 45
specialised in the spectacle of pantomime. Grimaldi became the most famous of pantomime clowns, pioneering the art of the cross-dressing dame with such characters as Queen Rondabellyana. 50

Pantomime is family entertainment, but it's not just aimed at kids. It's full of topical, political allusions and suggestive comments, which may be rude, but never offensive or abusive. If you want to experience English pantomime for yourself, 55
you'll find professional and amateur productions in just about every town during the winter season. So, if you're planning a winter trip to England, make sure to take in this historical entertainment. It's fun! 60

Section 1: Directed Writing

1. Imagine you are an American planning a visit to Britain. You have read about English pantomimes and would like to take your seven-year-old British nephew Simon and his twin sister Sofia to see *Cinderella* in London.

Write a letter to the children's parents asking permission to take them to the pantomime. Tell them what the children will see and why you think they will enjoy it. Add any other details you consider to be relevant. Write between 250 and 350 words. Start like this:

Dear Jonas and Trudy,

I'm coming to England in December and ...

Use a separate sheet of paper if necessary.

....
....
....
....
....
....
....
....
....
....
....
....
....
....
....
....
....
....
....
....
....
....
....
....
....
....

Section 2: Composition

Write between 350 and 450 words on one of the following:

2. **Descriptive writing**

   a. Describe the scene and atmosphere in a bus station, train station or airport where you or other people are setting out on a long journey.

   OR

   b. Describe a place of refuge or safe retreat.

   OR

3. **Narrative writing**

   a. "I don't believe it!" Write a story in which a character cannot believe what he/she sees.

   OR

   b. Write the closing scene of a story in which a character is in danger and time is running out.

   Use a separate sheet of paper if necessary.

....

....

....

....

....

....

....

....

....

....

....

....

....

....

....

....

....

....

....